THE FLORIDA PROJECT

21ST CENTURY FILM ESSENTIALS

Cinema has a storied history, but its story is far from over. *21ˢᵗ Century Film Essentials* offers a lively chronicle of cinema's second century, examining the landmark films of our ever-changing moment. Each book makes a case for the importance of a particular contemporary film for artistic, historical, or commercial reasons. The twenty-first century has already been a time of tremendous change in filmmaking the world over, from the rise of digital production and the ascent of the multinational blockbuster to increased vitality in independent filmmaking and the emergence of new voices and talents both on screen and off. The films examined here are the ones that embody and exemplify these changes, crystallizing emerging trends or pointing in new directions. At the same time, they are films that are informed by and help refigure the cinematic legacy of the previous century, showing how film's past is constantly reimagined and rewritten by its present. These are films both familiar and obscure, foreign and domestic; they are new but of lasting value. This series is a study of film history in the making. It is meant to provide a different kind of approach to cinema's story—one written in the present tense.

Donna Kornhaber, Series Editor

Also in the Series

Patrick Keating, *Harry Potter and the Prisoner of Azkaban*
Dana Polan, *The LEGO Movie*

The Florida Project

Project

J. J. Murphy

UNIVERSITY OF TEXAS PRESS ✦ AUSTIN

Requests for permission to reproduce material from
this work should be sent to:
    Permissions
    University of Texas Press
    P.O. Box 7819
    Austin, TX 78713-7819
    utpress.utexas.edu/rp-form

♾ The paper used in this book meets the minimum requirements
of ANSI/NISO Z39.48-1992 (R1997) (Permanence of Paper).

Library of Congress Cataloging-in-Publication Data

Names: Murphy, J. J., 1947– author.
Title: The Florida project / J. J. Murphy.
Description: First edition. | Austin : University of Texas Press, 2021. |
    Series: 21st century film essentials | Includes bibliographical references
    and index.
Identifiers: LCCN 2021007057
    ISBN 978-1-4773-2404-2 (paperback)
    ISBN 978-1-4773-2405-9 (PDF)
    ISBN 978-1-4773-2406-6 (ePub)
Subjects: LCSH: Baker, Sean, 1971– | Florida project (Motion picture) |
    Independent films. | Independent films—Case studies.
Classification: LCC PN1997.2.F64 M87 2021 | DDC 791.43/72—dc23
LC record available at https://lccn.loc.gov/2021007057

doi:10.7560/324042

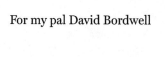

For my pal David Bordwell

Contents

THE FLORIDA PROJECT

Introduction

Sean Baker's career as an independent filmmaker has been on a steady upward trajectory for the past fifteen years. Each new film has represented a distinct advance over the previous one. Although Baker's films had already achieved a great deal of critical acclaim within indie circles, there was not much pre-festival buzz when *Tangerine* (2015), a film he improbably shot with an iPhone 5s, debuted in the more experimental Next section at the Sundance Film Festival. Yet *Tangerine* wound up becoming one of the most talked about films of the festival, was picked up for distribution by Magnolia Pictures, and made seven times its budget at the box office. Baker's next film, *The Florida Project* (2017), featuring Willem Dafoe, also exceeded expectations. The film premiered at the Director's Fortnight at the Cannes Film Festival, was acquired by *Moonlight* (2016) distributor A24, and grossed nearly $11 million worldwide.[1] *The Florida Project*, in effect, established Sean Baker as one of America's top indie filmmakers working today.

Remarking on the origins of his interest in film, Baker recalls, "My mother took me to the local library at six-years-old to watch clips from Universal monster films. I remember the sound of the projector. The burning mill sequence at the end of James Whale's *Frankenstein* made me want to become a director. The internal mechanics of the windmill as it's being looked through instantaneously struck me as the best thing

I'd ever seen."[2] His early childhood reminiscence of being enthralled by the sensory aspects of cinema is hardly surprising given the keen sense of a child's view of the world that imbues *The Florida Project*. Much of the pleasure in watching the film entails observing the buoyant behavior of its mischievous six-year-old protagonist, Moonee, who lives with her struggling single mom, Halley, in one of the budget motels in the shadow of Walt Disney World.

Even walking around the motel grounds and surrounding area becomes an adventure for Moonee and her friends, Scooty and Jancey, as they contort their lithe bodies like Gumby, break into improvised dance moves, amuse themselves by making farting sounds, imagine being on a safari in a cow pasture, chase a giant rainbow, or give middle fingers to the noisy helicopters that continually take off and fly overhead for short tours of Disney World. Early in the film, the three of them walk along the highway strip past kitschy gift shops—one in the form of a giant orange, the other an immense wizard—to the Twistee Treat, where they beg money from tourists to buy ice cream. To watch Moonee and her pals eat a single vanilla cone is one of the film's delights. Each child sucks or licks or kisses the ice cream with great panache. Such scenes trigger memories in viewers of what it was like to experience the world so vividly—something that Stan Brakhage attempted to replicate in a number of his avant-garde films, most notably *Scenes from Under Childhood* (1967–1970).

Alexis Zabé's cinematography and Stephonik Youth's production design emphasize the sensory wonders of childhood through their meticulous use of a vibrant color palette, which Baker describes as "pop verité." Baker contrasts a child's perceptual view of the world—much of the film is shot from low

Sean Baker and crew shooting the scene of Moonee, Scooty, and Jancey eating ice cream at the Twistee Treat. Photo courtesy of A24 Distribution, LLC.

angles—with the grim social conditions of the budget motels that house homeless families: fistfights, drug use, sexual predators, transient friendships, and brutal violence. All of this will have a deep emotional impact on these young children and shape their futures, just as the burning mill sequence in *Frankenstein* left an indelible imprint on Baker and influenced his subsequent choice to become a film director.

The British director Ken Loach insists, "The way you make a film is an important way of validating the ideas in it."[3] In Baker's uncompromising fictional portrait of homeless kids growing up in budget motels, he employed an unconventional approach that was aligned with his subject matter—a somewhat risky strategy for a larger-budget indie film being shot with a union crew. These strategies included alternative scripting, unorthodox casting of local and first-time actors, the use of various forms of improvisation, team-like collaboration, a guerrilla-like mode of filmmaking, an episodic story structure, and a blend of documentary and fiction rooted in what Baker himself refers to as "social realism."

The screenplay for *The Florida Project* remained in a state of flux throughout both preproduction and production. Normally a complete screenplay becomes the means to obtain financing and to start putting a film package together, but that turned out not to be the case in this instance. It was not as if nothing existed on paper—there was a short scriptment (a cross between a script and treatment) to show potential financiers—but Baker's method of filmmaking is not dependent on having a completed script. Although a "final" version of the shooting script only appeared at the very start of production, certain scenes and one of the major characters had yet to be determined. Even more confounding is the fact that the actual ending of the film still remained an open question, and major changes to the screenplay would continue to be made in the midst of production.

The casting of the film posed a dilemma. Baker believed that using well-known professional actors or major stars would not be believable to viewers of a film about the hidden homeless, so he was looking to discover first-time actors or new faces who would be closer in real life to his characters. Baker was intent on casting the child performers locally. Despite hiring casting agents, finding the right four children within the confines of Florida turned out to be a significant challenge. Street casting eventually enabled him to locate first-time actors to play Scooty and Jancey, but discovering a child actor to play the key role of Moonee proved to be even more difficult. Casting first-time and inexperienced actors that he found online to play the major roles of Halley and Ashley (Scooty's mother) represented another bold decision on Baker's part. It might be assumed that Willem Dafoe was the very first person cast and part of the financing package, but this wasn't the case. Even more surprising is the fact that another professional actor, Caleb Landry Jones, was chosen after production was already underway and his character finally had been decided upon.

That the screenplay for *The Florida Project* remained a continual work in progress has largely to do with the fact that Baker implicitly believes in improvisation as a means of keeping the energy of a film both fresh and alive. In his book *Improvising Cinema*, Gilles Mouëllic emphasizes the tentative nature of the process of artistic creation for improvisers: "The improvising filmmaker is not seeking the perfection of a completed work, but the demonstration of a work-in-progress, and he views the creative process as a journey, or even a sketch or draft."[4] Locations, the actors, serendipitous events and situations, and what might actually be occurring in the moment all shaped Baker's decisions in scripting and production. Working with very young child actors meant that written lines often proved untenable, which is why Baker eventually gave up having them stick to the written words of the script. Mouëllic suggests the connection between the methods of improvisation and documentary filmmaking, noting that "the aim is always to destabilise the fiction and produce unforeseen effects of reality."[5]

Although critics and scholars recognize that films are by their very nature collective endeavours, auteurism still holds sway, especially in indic cinema. Yet, among indie filmmakers,

Baker is somewhat unique in his steadfast commitment to working collaboratively. He relies on input from a small inner circle of trusted collaborators in key positions to understand his vision and help translate it onto the screen. Many of his collaborators have producing credits as a recognition of what they contribute to the realization of the final film.

Up until *The Florida Project*, Baker spent his entire career making indie films on shoestring budgets. He developed a guerilla style of filmmaking in which he was forced to shoot on location, cast first-time actors, and devise techniques that were more akin to how a documentary filmmaker works. Small budgets have their downside, but having little money also affords a filmmaker greater freedom and flexibility to work spontaneously. A larger budget, such as Baker had for the first time on *The Florida Project*, changed the equation. A bare-bones crew suddenly shifted into a much larger and more unwieldy one, with strict rules governing how everything needed to be done. Baker's impromptu style of following his own impulses and making changes on the spot wound up rankling some professional crew members, causing a major crisis during the shooting of a feature already plagued by scheduling delays.

The Florida Project has an unusual dramatic act structure: a very long first act (48.5 minutes), a shorter middle act (40 minutes), and an extremely short final act (20 minutes). It's not that Baker doesn't understand narrative pacing or know how to tell a story in the classical Hollywood sense; rather, he believes that doing so would not be true to the story world of homeless children and their parents living in the budget motels. Baker views fiction in a similar way to Ken Loach. In discussing characters, Loach observes, "It's about how they live in their rooms, how they've got the food they put on their table. It's about the fabric of life, the product of all those details of the way we are. Politics is implicit in all that, but it can't be dragged out of it."[6]

Through a more observational approach, Baker is interested in capturing those types of everyday details that define his characters, especially in the first act, rather than in having a tight and predictable dramatic structure. Yet several unexpected narrative events and situations do occur in the film, such as when a major character disappears entirely from the story early on. In his interactions with his son, the good-hearted motel manager, Bobby, is suddenly revealed in a new light. The arc of Halley's character shifts unexpectedly as her circumstances become more desperate. And fantasy suddenly blurs with reality for Moonee once Halley's actions invite retribution.

Baker is one of the most socially concerned and political contemporary American indie filmmakers, which is why he is drawn to social realism. Historically, the term "social realism" has its roots in documentary film, Italian Neorealism, and, more particularly, British social realism. The category is often applied to British New Wave films from the period 1958–1963, such as Tony Richardson's *Look Back in Anger* (1959) and Karel Reitz's *Saturday Night and Sunday Morning* (1960), as well as later films by Ken Loach and Mike Leigh, two directors Baker often cites as important influences on his own work.

"Social realism" is a broad term. The same could be said for "realism," which is also a highly mutable and time-based concept. As Samantha Lay argues, "What is regarded as 'real', by whom, and how it is represented is unstable, dynamic, and ever-changing, precisely because realism is irrevocably tied to the specifics of time and place, or 'moment.'"[7] Social realist films exhibit certain characteristics. First and foremost, these fiction films are intended to be an oppositional practice to mainstream Hollywood cinema. Although social realist films explore a diversity of artistic approaches, they generally strive to reflect actuality, focus on characters from marginal or underrepresented groups, exhibit a tight nexus between character and place, and deal with relevant issues that grow out of their particular social milieu.

Julia Hallam and Margaret Marshment define "social realism" as "a discursive term used by film critics and reviewers to describe films that aim to show the effects of environmental factors on the development of character through depictions that emphasise the relationship between location and identity."[8] In cinema, locations are not simply neutral backdrops for either dialogue or action. Place can not only affect a narrative but also give rise to it. Although the terms "location" and "place" are often used more or less interchangeably, there is, in fact, a critical difference between them. All fiction films utilize locations—either found or constructed—as a setting for the narrative. After all, in the formatting of traditional screenplays, the location is included as part of the standard heading of a scene. The term "on location" also indicates that a film is shot in an actual existing setting rather than on a set. "Location" suggests a geographical coordinate, whereas "place" has cultural, historical, and personal implications. "Place" is more resonant; it implies a location or setting that elicits a specific or unique identity or personality. As a result, place can become a crucial element in a narrative film.

A central tenet of social realism is the notion that the places characters inhabit within a story world can very much influence and define their behavior. Glorianna Davenport of the

Media Lab at MIT writes, "Narratives 'take place' as characters converge, act, and interact within the framework of a specific place and time. 'Place' immerses characters in a situated context where details of history, culture, and the available physical affordances provide opportunities and constraints that influence the choice of actions and interactions."[9] Davenport goes on to add, "In narrative worlds, places often manifest an approximation of personality and functional psychology in support of the story."[10] In other words, place can also function as "character." Baker concurs. In discussing his selection of the purple Magic Castle Inn as a main setting for *The Florida Project*, he comments, "For me, a place becomes a character."[11] This is true of Baker's films more generally, but especially of *The Florida Project*.

Baker is an avid cinephile. While many filmmakers often attempt to disguise their influences, he seems to exult in detailing them in various interviews. Baker often emphasizes filmmakers from international art cinema because of their alternate form of narration and eschewal of three-act structure, yet his work can easily be contextualized within the tradition of American indie cinema. An important strain of indie filmmakers has been drawn to naturalism, improvisation, and a sense of place from the early days of the New American Cinema, when filmmakers such as Morris Engel and Ruth Orkin, Lionel Rogosin, John Cassavetes, Kent Mackenzie, and Shirley Clarke borrowed from a documentary aesthetic to create an alternative to what they saw as the overly staged and scripted quality of the Hollywood studio film.

Using the bare frame of a story, Morris Engel and Ruth Orkin's *Little Fugitive* (1953) explores the legendary Brooklyn amusement park Coney Island through the eyes of an impressionable seven-year-old runaway. In making *On the Bowery* (1956), Lionel Rogosin spent six months observing life on Skid Row and getting to know the inhabitants of the Bowery in Lower Manhattan, as well as casting them in his film. The documentary images of the Bowery's denizens, such as those captured in the Mission scene, are as central to the film as the slim narrative. Kent Mackenzie hung out with the American Indians who inhabited the Bunker Hill section of Los Angeles and incorporated them into a film, *The Exiles* (1961), which he based on their lives.

A similar place-based realism also informs contemporary indie cinema, as exemplified by such films as Ramin Bahrani's *Chop Shop* (2007), Lance Hammer's *Ballast* (2008), Matthew Porterfield's *Putty Hill* (2010), Sam Fleischner's *Stand Clear of the Closing Doors* (2013), Eliza Hittman's *It Felt Like Love* (2013) and *Beach Rats* (2017), Kogonada's *Columbus* (2017), and Josh and Benny Safdie's *Heaven Knows What* (2014), *Good Time* (2017), and *Uncut Gems* (2019). Many American indie films remain rooted in a regional aesthetic that attempts to capture what is distinctive about a particular place.

Baker approaches each film like an ethnographer. He begins with an idea for a project, which is invariably tied to a particular urban location or place: a Chinese takeout restaurant, the wholesale district in Manhattan, the porn industry in the San Fernando Valley, the transgender prostitution district in the area around Donut Time in Los Angeles, or the homeless motels outside of Disney World. He spends a great deal of time researching and immersing himself in both the location and the subject, often relying on inside informants, some of whom he casts as actors in the film.

Baker allows the story to grow organically from the particular place rather than imposing it from without, using his considerable storytelling skills to fictionalize pressing social issues inherent in the marginalized subculture: the plight of undocumented workers, the underground economy of knockoff luxury goods, the problems of young sex workers in the adult film industry, the world of transgender prostitutes, or the lives of the hidden homeless families in motels on the outskirts of Disney World in Orlando. Baker explains, "All I can say is: I go into these stories not imposing a script or thought. I find the people from these worlds that I can connect and collaborate with. That, to me, is the only responsible way for any storyteller to tell a story—it's not right otherwise."[12]

Digital technology has managed to transform filmmaking in the twenty-first century. Baker's use of an iPhone to shoot *Tangerine* is a major example. The iPhone enabled him to shoot the ending of *The Florida Project* clandestinely at Disney World, and he was able to alter certain shots through CGI (computer-generated imagery) in postproduction. Social media also allowed Baker to broaden his search for actors. Although digital technology has democratized filmmaking by making the means of production more accessible, finding a wider audience for indie films has become an even bigger problem in an age of blockbusters and media conglomerates.

The production of *The Florida Project* presented a very difficult challenge for Baker. After years of struggling to make low-budget films, Baker was finally given a much larger budget for *The Florida Project*. Attempting to work on a larger scale often involves a tradeoff. Larger budgets bring greater financial risks, which create additional pressures on a production, with the result being that the films usually end up becoming more conventional. As a socially engaged filmmaker, Baker was determined not to compromise his vision of a film about the hidden homeless. Yet his aesthetic of social realism, flexible approach to scripting, reliance on improvisation, and penchant for employing guerrilla tactics often put him at odds with the cold reality of industrial filmmaking in such areas as casting, insurance, permits, and working with a professional union crew.

Although *The Florida Project* ended up being recognized as a remarkable artistic achievement by critics, the making of the film nevertheless serves as something of a cautionary tale. The transition to having a much larger budget and crew resulted in creative constraints on how Baker was used to working: "The film had to feel intimate. It was a character piece and not plot heavy, so it was more about small moments. And to keep the authenticity of that, you really have to try to have your footprint remain as small as possible, which is hard with a 40-person crew."[13] In many ways, the story of *The Florida Project* provides an emblematic case study of the opportunities but also the real tensions and pitfalls that indie filmmakers face in the evolving media landscape of the new century.

Origins of the Film

BAKER'S CAREER AND TRAJECTORY

Born on February 26, 1971, Sean Baker grew up in Short Hills and Branchburg, New Jersey. As a result of his fascination with the aesthetic power of combining images and sound, he began making his own Super 8 films and videos as a kid. Baker studied film production at the Tisch School for the Arts at NYU. He was scheduled to graduate with his class in 1992 but found himself one course short. Rather than finish the course—he didn't complete his BFA degree until 1998—he took a job in the industry in order to hone his production skills.

Baker worked at a publishing company, Multimedia Communicators, where he made promotional and industrial videos and gained a great deal of hands-on experience working with both audio and editing. He also made three TV commercials on the side. For one of them, which was shot in Super 16 mm, he was given a substantial budget of $50,000. Baker, however, was able to make it cheaply, which enabled him to save the rest of the money to put toward his first feature, *Four Letter Words* (2000), which he shot on leftover 35 mm film stock that he purchased directly from the production company that made Terry Gilliam's *Twelve Monkeys* (1995).[1] His career ambitions, however, became sidetracked for a number of years by an addiction to drugs—something he first spoke about publicly in November 2017, to *The Guardian*—before he was finally able to turn his life around.[2]

Baker's problems with drugs began in late 1994 or early 1995 and lasted until very early 2000. Before *Four Letter Words* he was "secretly dabbling," but his usage escalated into a full-blown problem once the film was shot. As he puts it, "After [the shooting of] *Four Letter Words*, it all went to hell."[3] After syncing the rushes all summer, by the time the cutting began in the fall of 1996, taking drugs had become a "semi-habit."

As the *Greg the Bunny* TV show began to "get legs" in 1997, Baker was still using, and after a year on the Independent Film Channel, he was let go by his two partners. This had the effect of further isolating him. Baker largely credits his relationship with Shih-Ching Tsou—she's thanked at the end of *Four Letter Words*—and his strong ambition to make films with helping him get through the serious life crisis he experienced during his twenties. Baker says, "I lost a lot of time. That's why, when you look at my peers, they're 10 years younger than me. I went through it hard. But I had support from people close to me, and from NA [Narcotics Anonymous]. And I was lucky enough to get out."[4]

Baker's *Four Letter Words* was begun in 1996 but took four years to complete, mostly due to editing problems and his own personal issues. Even though he learned a great deal, Baker now considers it a mistake that he insisted on editing the film on a 35 mm Steenbeck, which made the editing much more difficult. Shot in the Riverdale section of the Bronx, with additional locations in suburban Long Island and New Jersey, the film is about a group of college students who drink excessively and get high at an all-night summer party. A fight breaks out and one of the guys steals a case of Coca-Cola from the local gas station, but the film is otherwise rooted in the conversations of its multiple protagonists. The film is an examination of male culture, as the young men discuss getting laid, porn, sexual preferences, and the pervasive influence of Disney.

Compared to Baker's later films, *Four Letter Words* is dialogue-heavy rather than visual. The film contains very little plot. It uses parallel editing to crosscut between different conversations that develop among the men as the night progresses. As is typical of male culture, there is a lot of brash posturing among the friends. Most of them appear still fixated on high school, as if college has not had any impact on them. In that sense, the young men remain perpetually stuck in immature adolescence. There are moments, however, in which their masks come off and the friends actually seem to communicate with each other. One memorable scene occurs when Art (Fred Berman) and Noah (David Prete) get high together. Noah recognizes that Art has the potential to be a successful lawyer or doctor and have a nice, comfortable life.

The interaction is one that resembles scenes from the later mumblecore films of Joe Swanberg and Andrew Bujalski in its overriding sense of naturalism. It does not feel as scripted as other scenes and appears more spontaneous and improvised, with pauses occurring naturally as the two characters speak, so that facial and physical reactions become as important as their dialogue. Although *Four Letter Words* had a script, Baker actually constructed the film using a "rehearsed" form of improvisation.[5]

Prior to writing the script, Baker spent a couple of years making audio recordings of the conversations of his friends. The recorded dialogue was then transcribed into a script. Once the actors were cast through auditions, the first draft became

the basis for the actors to improvise during a six-month re-
hearsal period. The improvisations were videotaped, and the
best material was then transcribed into new versions of the
script. Due to the fact that the film was shot on 35 mm film,
which made filming expensive, the actors were expected to
adhere to the final script. The shoot lasted twenty-two days,
but additional reshoots were needed. In the bonus material
about the making of *Four Letter Words*, Baker indicates that
his "number-one goal on this film was to capture reality," which
is why he insisted that the vomiting scene involving Florio
(David Ari) could not be faked.[6]

Four Letter Words (originally titled *Climax*) was pro-
grammed by Matt Dentler and premiered at the SXSW Film
Festival in 2001, where four years later films that became
known as mumblecore would come to prominence and the
catchy moniker would first be coined. In introducing the film
at the festival, Baker told the audience that the film was based
on recordings he had made of conversations in college and
at parties. He stated that his "goal was to make a film that
accurately depicted suburban men in their early twenties."[7]
Dentler, who became one of the leading promoters of mumblecore, later told Baker that he considers *Four Letter Words*
to be "one of the first mumblecore films."[8]

If there is a difference, it has to do with the fact that Baker
insisted that his actors stick to the script once it was written,
which gives some of the scenes a more "acted" quality that
proves at odds with his intentions for the film. Baker attributes the idea of a "locked script" to his being influenced at the
time by what he understood to be the process of Mike Leigh.
Reflecting back on this inflexibility, he comments, "I'm now
100 percent the other way. I encourage improvisation. I try to

get as many alternate takes as possible to play with in post-production. So I learned that I didn't like that style by making *Four Letter Words*."[9]

Baker was also never happy with the final cut of *Four Letter Words*, so he recently recut and restored the film. Looking back, Baker notes, "I knew that I had gone in a wrong direction with the film to make it a *Rashomon*-type, three-story structure. And I never had the resources until literally twenty years later to really do it the way I wanted to do it."[10] The recut version is expected to be re-released in 2021.

With two collaborators, Spencer Chinoy and Dan Milano, Baker created a show entitled *Junktape*, which aired biweekly on a public-access cable channel in Manhattan. Segments of that, which mixed puppets and live action, became *The Greg the Bunny Show*, which aired on the Independent Film Channel. The show was subsequently acquired by the Fox channel and became *Greg the Bunny* (2002), but the series was canceled after the first year. In 2005, the show returned to the IFC with a series of short segments that spoofed both old and new movies. Along with his two collaborators, Baker created a spinoff of *Greg the Bunny* entitled *Warren the Ape* (2010). The show appeared on MTV, but also ended up being canceled after a single season. Yet the experience of working in TV resulted in certain career benefits for Baker. One was that it gave him an opportunity to experiment with improvisation. In addition, his commercial TV work funded his next three low-budget, independent features.[11]

Baker spent the time between *Four Letter Words* and his next film watching a lot of films. He was especially inspired by the work of Lars von Trier and Dogme 95. He also gained a lot of confidence in himself during this time and matured as a result of developing a number of close personal relationships. Stylistically, *Four Letter Words* is something of an anomaly in relation to Baker's subsequent work. In returning to making independent features, Baker recalibrated his approach to filmmaking by shifting his emphasis toward social realism. His second feature, *Take Out* (2004–2008), which he codirected with Shih-Ching Tsou on a budget of $3,000, grew out of their experience of living above a Chinese restaurant.

The film explores the subculture of undocumented Chinese immigrants in telling the story of a delivery person, Ming Ding (Charles Jang), who is given twenty-four hours to repay his debts to loan sharks. The biggest changes for Baker were relying less on a script and incorporating techniques that were more typical of a documentary shooting style. Baker filmed on the streets of Manhattan, using a busy Chinese takeout restaurant on the Upper West Side during business hours as his main set and recruiting the owner of the shop, Feng Lin, and various customers to play themselves. Although the film found a small distributor, Cavu Pictures, five years passed before *Take Out* finally had a theatrical release.

The attraction of shooting in a specific location—in this case, the energetic "wholesale" district in Manhattan—became the inspiration for Baker's next feature, *Prince of Broadway* (2008), which was produced and cowritten by Darren Dean. Baker spent a year researching the neighborhood, where counterfeit luxury goods were sold on the streets and in the backrooms of the numerous shops that lined Broadway between Twenty-Sixth and Thirtieth Streets. Baker was referred to a local street peddler named Prince Adu, who, it turned out, had aspirations to act in movies. In return for being cast in the lead role as Lucky, Adu became Baker's principal informant and helped to provide access to the world of another immigrant community, the West Africans who eked out a living in the underground economy of this neighborhood.[12]

Baker had already planned to cast Karren Karagulian, an Armenian actor who had appeared in *Four Letter Words*, as one of the customers in *Take Out*. In terms of storytelling, Baker used the story of Lucky having a baby thrust upon him by a vindictive girlfriend to create the central dramatic conflict. A paternity test provides the ticking clock for the story. Baker and Dean created various scenes for the film, but the actors were allowed to improvise their own dialogue. *Prince of Broadway* won major prizes at the Locarno Film Festival, Los Angeles Film Festival, and Torino Film Festival. The combination of *Prince of Broadway* and *Take Out* brought attention to Baker within indie film circles, especially when both films were nominated for the 2009 John Cassavetes Independent Spirit Award for films made with budgets of less than $500,000.

Sean Baker began to seem like the quintessential New York City indie filmmaker following the releases of *Take Out* and *Prince of Broadway*, but he then spent a year in Los Angeles working on *Warren the Ape*, where he conceived of the idea for his next film. He returned to New York in 2011 to write the film and then relocated permanently to Los Angeles to shoot *Starlet* (2012), which once again deals with characters living on the margins of society. The film, which Baker cowrote with Chris Bergoch, stars the model and actor Dree Hemingway as a young woman named Jane, and Besedka Johnson, an octogenarian first-time actor, as Sadie.

The two characters develop an incongruous relationship after Jane buys a thermos that turns out to contain a large amount of money at Sadie's yard sale. The film only gradually reveals that Jane works in the porn business. Baker shot *Starlet* in actual locations connected to the adult film industry in the San Fernando Valley. The setting, however, contributes more than just an intriguing backdrop to the story. It actually provides a crucial context for establishing the relationships between the various characters, as well as the motivation behind why Jane might be drawn to someone like Sadie. In exposing the less glamorous underside of this stigmatized social milieu, Baker shows how it shapes young women who get trapped emotionally in what he describes as a kind of dependent "pre-adolescent environment."[13] We come to see that, like Jane's male Chihuahua, Starlet, Sadie represents a kind of desperate lifeline.

Baker hoped his next film would be a much bigger-budget project, but he was not interested in working as a director for hire. Victoria Tate had worked as a research partner with Baker on *Prince of Broadway* and played Levon's wife, Nadia, in the film. She and Baker cowrote a screenplay that was set in Brighton Beach. According to Peter Broderick in *IndieWire*, "It looked like his script 'Caviar' about the Russian-Armenian underworld in Brooklyn was going to be financed for between $10 and $15 million. After waiting 1½ years for the money to arrive, Baker decided he would have to return to the world of micro-budget filmmaking."[14] He took the Duplass brothers up on their open offer to finance a film for $100,000, which resulted in his making *Tangerine*, using an iPhone 5s as a cost-saving device.

Tangerine centered on Donut Time on the corner of Highland and Santa Monica Boulevard in Los Angeles. The small shop, and the colorful characters who frequented it, became the inspiration for him to make a film about transgender prostitution. In researching the surrounding neighborhood, Baker met an aspiring transgender actor named Mya Taylor who provided entry to this world and introduced him to Kitana Kiki Rodriguez. Baker and Bergoch developed the scriptment for the film in stages. They began with a brief outline that the writers proceeded to develop in rehearsals with the two first-time actors.

The story takes place on Christmas Eve and involves the friendship between Alexandra (Taylor) and her highly volatile friend, Sin-Dee Rella (Rodriguez), who meet at Donut Time following Sin-Dee's release from prison. Alexandra's revelation that Sin-Dee's pimp boyfriend, Chester (James Ransone), has cheated on her sets the main plot in motion, involving an Armenian taxicab driver named Razmik who regularly cruises the neighborhood as part of his secret life away from his wife and child. *Tangerine* became Baker's most popular and highest grossing film to date. Its critical success gave him newfound currency; what project would Baker choose next?

DEVELOPMENT OF THE SCREEN IDEA

Ian Macdonald has introduced the concept of the "screen idea" as a useful analytical approach in contemporary screenwriting studies. Macdonald defines the term as "any notion held by one or more people of a singular concept (however complex), which may have conventional shape or not, intended to become a screenwork, whether or not it is possible to describe it in written form or by other means."[15] The screen idea helps us to understand that scripting is a dynamic and collective process that undergoes transformation through the various stages of preproduction and production as well as editing and postproduction. According to Macdonald:

> The simple notion of the screen idea allows us to talk of what lies behind what is on screen—beliefs as well as practice; what individuals or teams are contributing; what institutional structures relate to their activities; how orthodoxies and common norms are (or are not) applied, how society is represented; how issues of political economy interact, not just with production in a technical sense, but with the initial conception of appropriate production.[16]

The concept has particular relevance to understanding Sean Baker's work, especially *The Florida Project*, as a result of the director's highly collaborative and unorthodox method of making films.

Macdonald also discusses what he terms a Screen Idea Work Group (SIWG), a collaborative unit consisting of "everyone who contributes something to the development of the screen idea, whatever their professional title."[17] Macdonald explains, "There is a core membership of stakeholders with decision-making powers, including the acknowledged leader, and a looser membership of contributors; the division between these is flexible and may change."[18] On *The Florida Project*, there was a core team, or SIWG, but it did not fit the traditional model seen in most commercial or independent films. As director, Baker had free rein to make creative decisions on the film, including the contractual guarantee of "final cut," but the SIWG he assembled, as we will see, helped to shape the final film in innumerable and complex ways.

The development of the screen idea for *The Florida Project* began with Baker's co-screenwriter, Chris Bergoch, who grew up in New Jersey but had been going to Walt Disney World since he was a child. While visiting his mother, who had moved to Kissimmee, Florida, he noticed the large number of children playing on the streets near the motels on his way back and forth to visit the theme park. When he spoke to his mother about what he had noticed, she was aware of the problem, which already had been publicized in the local media. Through additional research, Bergoch learned more about the economic and social transformation taking place on the outskirts of Disney World.

The Great Recession, which began in December of 2007, caused an unprecedented spike in the homeless population in the United States. Particularly affected by the economic malaise that gripped the country were young families and children. Alexandra Pelosi's HBO documentary *Homeless: The Kids of Orange County* (2010) helped bring public attention to the predicament of homeless children living in motels on the outskirts of Disneyland in California.

Although the problem is national in scope, Florida has the third largest number of homeless people in the country. The situation became especially acute in Central Florida, where the construction industry collapsed and foreclosures left many families homeless. Housing simply became unaffordable for those with low-wage jobs or those unable to find any employment at all. The tourism industry, which lured many people to the area, often did not pay its employees enough money to enable them to rent an apartment, forcing many families to live on the streets or in their cars, or to seek temporary shelter in nearby budget motels.

Starting around 2011, a series of newspaper and magazine articles, as well as a TV segment on CBS's *60 Minutes* entitled "Hard Times Generation: Homeless Kids," publicized the acute plight of homeless families, including those living in the seedy hotels in Central Florida. The TV program focuses on one family with three children in Seminole County who were forced to live in their car, which was parked at night in a Walmart lot. In the morning, the two older kids had to use the bathroom at the discount store in order to get ready for school. The family eventually moved into two rooms in a motel. The rest of their possessions were put in storage, but these were all lost when the family could not afford to make the rental payments. As a result, the kids lost many of their possessions, including clothes, a scooter, a video game console, toys, and Barbie dolls.

The next segment of the program focuses on the area surrounding Disney World, the supposed "happiest place on earth." It reports that five hundred children are living in sixty-seven motels along the Highway 192 corridor in Kissimmee leading to the theme park. Included in the montage of motels is the Paradise Motel, whose sign was transformed by the production designer into that of the Futureland Motel in *The Florida Project*. According to the TV exposé, a thousand children are homeless in Orange County, Florida. A series of interviews with children who don't have enough food to eat provide a heartbreaking portrait. Families often must choose between food and electricity, making it difficult for the children to study at night.

An interview with a teacher suggests that the problem of impoverished children keeps growing, putting their futures at risk. A mother faced with homelessness suggests the vital importance of keeping the family together no matter where they are. As her teenage son explains, "As long as you're with your family, you are going to make it through all of this that's been going on. All of it." Yet the homeless families are continually faced with the threat of separation. As opposed to a shelter, a motel at least temporarily permits the families to stay together as a unit.[19]

In one highly influential article that appeared on April 19, 2012, in the *Huffington Post*, Saki Knafo, citing statistics from the US Department of Education, estimated that there were at least two thousand children living in the hotels of Central Florida. According to Knafo, homeless advocates claim that "the hotel is to the modern American family what the city shelter was to the homeless adult of the 1980s and the migrant camp was to the refugees of the Oklahoma dust storms."[20] The author describes the phenomenon:

> Families make up the fast-growing segment of America's homeless population. Thousands live in hotels. The Department of Education has identified 47,000 hotel kids in schools around the country, and says that the number of homeless kids in public schools has increased by 38 percent since 2007. In Central Florida, it isn't uncommon to hear of 19 or 20 hotel kids in a class of 22 at the local schools.[21]

Knafo discusses the impact of instability on the lives of children. Being forced to move constantly—sometimes as many as four times a year—causes them to fall behind in school. It results in enormous stress that causes anxiety and depression. Children who are raised poor replicate the bad decision-making of their parents, which leads to a cycle that begins to perpetuate itself. Knafo observes, "Bringing up a child in the chaotic conditions of poverty must be something like building a skyscraper on quicksand. Instability begets instability begets instability."[22]

In an email dated April 20, 2012, one day after Knafo's *Huffington Post* article appeared, Bergoch pitches the possibility of making a film dealing with the subject to Baker. He describes his idea for "a film almost entirely set in a rundown motel filled with homeless families and other unmagical elements and shady characters all in the shadow of the magic of Cinderella's castle."[23] After citing a link to Knafo's article, he continues, "It's actually very sad . . . I'm not sure what the story is here—maybe it revolves around one family in particular just trying to stay afloat in these hard times, seen through the eyes of one of the kids who is having this most unmagical lifestyle right in the middle of the tourist capital of America."[24] Bergoch emphasizes Highway 192 in terms of its filmic appeal:

> My Mom lives close to here; it's basically a giant ten mile strip of motels and junky souvenir stores on this roadway called [US Route] 192 . . . used to be thriving, now many are boarded up, kind of a ghost town, meth dealers taking over some of the motels not boarded up—terrible decline in last few years—the thought of kids living in these motels and making it has so much potential.[25]

Baker responds back the same day that he always wanted to make a Florida film and suggests coming up "with a plot that takes place in one of these hotels."[26] Bergoch answers the following day that he sees the new film "as more

of the gritty social-realism style" of *Prince of Broadway*.[27] He
envisions most of the movie taking place in one of these motels and mentions the Gator Motel as a possibility; he also
thinks there need to be other inhabitants of the motel as characters and references Spike Lee's *Do the Right Thing* (1989)
as a model. After thinking about it some more, he suggests
possibly having the film center on a love story between a boy
and a girl who is visiting as a tourist and has to leave at the
end. Bergoch also comes up with the idea of the kid "flipping
unused theme park tickets" (multi-day passes) as a scam to
make money. He again mentions his enthusiasm for the setting
of the film.[28] Because Baker often responded to Bergoch by
phone rather than email, the conversation between the two
screenwriters might appear to be one-sided.

In a subsequent email, dated April 23, Bergoch begins his
correspondence by coming up with a title for the proposed
film: "When Walt Disney was keeping his plans for WDW
under wraps, way before it opened in 1971, its code name was
'The Florida Project'... so that's what I will refer to this project
as from now on...." In suggesting another location, he adds,
"I have another amazing location idea that actually has to be
part of The Florida Project (that's actually not a bad actual
title because it has a double meaning!... not only in Walt's old
working title but also the motels are basically like inner-city
projects down here)!" Bergoch views the locations as helping
to create the story, indicating that this is how he wrote his
first scripts, using a series of locations to develop a story. He
loves the "abandoned and closed attractions" in Kissimmee.
He especially regrets that Xanadu House of the Future was
demolished in 2005, or it would certainly have been his top
choice for a location. He mentions that another one, Splendid

China, is still standing, so he provides Baker with a link to it and begins to imagine a sequence taking place there.

Bergoch throws out some brainstorming ideas involving the two main characters. He suggests switching the gender of the protagonist from male to female and then proposes that maybe the protagonist is a "little tom-boy girl." He muses about what sounds like a Hollywood pitch: "It can be *Do the Right Thing* meets *Little Manhattan* [2005]." Bergoch then returns to the importance of locations. He writes that most of it will "take place at the rundown motel and inside the rooms of it." But he suggests other possibilities, including "an old abandoned attraction—like 'Splendid China' or old closed castle attraction also on Rt. 192 perhaps." Others include a swampy area with possible alligators lurking and the "parking lot of one of the Disney parks," where the idea of flipping tickets to the theme park could occur.[29] On May 4, in reference to secret stories related to the death of parents, Baker sends Bergoch a link to an article in the *Daily Mail* dated May 29, 2008, about two children who lived alone and existed on junk food after their parents were jailed in Turkey.[30]

Bergoch and Baker quickly put together a short treatment for the new project. On May 27, Bergoch sent his writing partner a draft with two graphics. Space had been left for additional pictures to be included. Knafo's article from the *Huffington Post*, which was attached, provides the social and political context for the story, which is about a nine-year-old girl named Gin. She meets a boy of the same age from London named Hamlyn Davis who is visiting with his family. The two share adventures at Gin's retreat from the world: the abandoned tourist attraction Splendid China. The pitch explains, "A broken down, weed-infested mess to you and I, but through the eyes of this imaginative 9-year-old, it's the closest she can come to Never Never Land. To these two kids, it doesn't matter that the park is long closed, half demolished and overrun with bugs and wildlife—they have the time of their lives together."[31]

In a later, more complete version of the initial treatment, the story is essentially the same but more details have been added. It is about a homeless mother and her nine-year-old daughter who live in one of the budget motels, the Gator Motel. The daughter is again named Gin. It still involves a friendship between Gin and a young visiting tourist, but he has now become a German boy named Oswin who is staying with his parents at a nearby three-star motel. His father is there on a business trip to "flip" foreclosed real estate. Despite the fact that Oswin cannot speak English, the two kids meet and soon have a great time together. They explore the abandoned buildings and boarded-up theme parks resulting from the economic recession, such as Splendid China, and create their own sense of imaginative fun and adventure.

After seeing pictures of where Oswin lives in Cologne, Germany, Gin becomes so enamored with her new friend that she wants to return home with him. As a way to pay for her plane ticket, she borrows the idea behind the business transactions of Oswin's father and decides "to 'flip' theme park tickets." As Gin doggedly sells and resells Disney World tickets to tourists, she soon manages to accumulate enough money. But when Oswin tells his parents about her plan of going home with them, they become alarmed. The parents contact the police, who investigate and find Gin's mother dead in the bathtub. Gin has kept her mother's suicide a secret in order to avoid being sent to a foster family. Using the one remaining ticket left from her scam, she escapes into Disney World.

Included with the treatment are pictures of various motels and abandoned tourist attractions. There are pictures of the

Gator Motel and the Magic Castle, as well as an image of the Jungle Falls Gift Shop (whose facade is a giant wizard), which eventually appeared in the film. There's also a picture of a fire at one of the abandoned buildings. Included once again is the article from the *Huffington Post* detailing the homeless crisis along Highway 192. There is also an article about a scam that occurred at the Hard Rock Hotel in the Universal Resort in Orlando. According to the article, a thirty-year-old man was jailed for "sneaking into a hotel room and claiming he was the room's previous guest, then using the credit card on file to rack up thousands of dollars in charges."[32]

Although the story for *The Florida Project* remained largely unformed, attempts were made to pitch the idea to potential funders. There was a definite hook in the juxtaposition between the magical aura of Disney World and the number of homeless children living in the motels in the surrounding area, but Baker was never able to generate any real interest in the project. One of the biggest obstacles turned out to be the suicide of the mother at the end, which was deemed to be much too negative by virtually everyone who read it. Eventually, the release and popularity of Benh Zeitlin's *Beasts of the Southern Wild* (2012) made it very difficult for Baker to pitch *The Florida Project* to potential investors due to some similarities in content between the two. As a result, the project had to be put on temporary hold while Baker moved on to other film ideas and eventually made *Tangerine*.

When that film premiered at the Sundance Film Festival in January 2015 and created a great deal of buzz, Baker began to bat around ideas for his next project with his close-knit group of collaborators. It suddenly became much easier to obtain financing for a new project. Although Baker had a number of unproduced screenplays from which to draw, *The Florida Project* suddenly found new life. He was glad that the project had initially stalled because he realized that he needed a much larger budget to shoot the film, which now seemed like a viable possibility.

As is his usual practice, Baker began by doing extensive research. He and Bergoch relied on informants to assist them in learning about the subject of the homeless children living in motels. One major resource turned out to be the Reverend Mary Lee Downey, the head of the Community Hope Center in Kissimmee, or "Hope 192" as it is often called. The social services agency had been working with homeless families in the area since 2013. Because there are no shelters in Osceola County, many of the homeless end up populating the motels on Highway 192.

The issue of homeless families living in motels, according to Downey, stems from the lack of affordable housing in the area. She explains:

The reason why we have so many families in the motels and hotels is because first, there's not enough affordable housing. Second, when affordable housing becomes available, there are large barriers put in place so that people who are in the motels are not able to obtain that housing—they may have double evictions or very poor credit. So even though they may be paying $900 to $1,300 a month at a motel, they're not able to [get housing] because of their poor history.[33]

The generational issue of poverty begetting poverty cited by Knafo in his *Huffington Post* article is something that Downey also has witnessed firsthand. She observes, "I call it an epidemic, a catastrophe for our community because we should not be seeing generational poverty of children growing up in a hotel and seeing no other options for them but also being in a hotel."[34]

Downey put the screenwriters in touch with homeless families. Baker and Bergoch soon realized from their research that the initial story needed serious revision. After talking extensively with Downey, homeless families, and city officials about the myriad problems facing the homeless, the screenwriters realized that the issue was much more complex than they had initially understood. In writing the screenplay, Baker was intent on getting the politics of the story right.

The more the two screenwriters researched the subject, the heavier it became. Baker was interested in the sociopolitical aspects of the film but was always trying to walk a fine line by trying to approach it in a comedic way. The motels turned out to be no different from bad housing projects. The same sorts of problems, such as the presence of roaches and lice, prostitution, domestic abuse, sexual predators, and heavy drug use, were pervasive, making the motels a treacherous environment for young children. The screenwriters also found that meth labs were common within the motels housing the homeless. In 2010, for instance, a meth lab exploded in the Carefree Inn on Highway 192 in Kissimmee, sending two people to the hospital with burns.[35] Lice posed a real problem for the homeless kids living in the motels. They would also become an issue for Baker's crew members working in the environment of the motels during production, but he chose not to emphasize that problem, or the prevalent issue of hardcore drugs, in the film.

The two screenwriters talked with homeless advocates

in the area. They also spoke with homeless residents of the
motel as well as motel managers to learn as much as possible.
One of the managers became an important resource for developing Willem Dafoe's character. On a trip to Walmart prior to
shooting, the two screenwriters observed a mother having fun
pushing her daughter around in a shopping cart. The woman
became one of the informants on the project. In the mother
and daughter, the writers believed they had found the real-life
Halley and Moonee.[36] Since they had already written a similar
scene in the script, it gave them confidence that they were on
the right track in terms of the accuracy of their characterization.

The screenplay for the film, which was written over a
four-year period, underwent considerable changes in the process. In what is titled "an international pitch," Baker discusses
The Florida Project in terms of Hal Roach's *The Little Rascals*: " 'The Little Rascals: 2016.' This is how I like to describe
'The Florida Project.' For those who remember the 'Our Gang'
shorts of the 20's and 30's, they will know that, essentially,
these films focused on children who lived in poverty during the
Great Depression. But their economic state was the backdrop.
The children's humorous adventures were the focus."[37]

Although Baker wanted to create an engaging story about
kids, he spells out his political aspirations and the timeliness
of the film in great detail:

> Now is the perfect time to tell this story. The local gov-
> ernment is in the process of changing zoning laws in
> the Kissimmee/Orlando area. Families with children
> who have little chance at dwelling elsewhere are having
> yet another option taken away. Laws are now requir-
> ing these motels and hotels to evict or refuse service to

families who are officially homeless—the whole reason
they are forced to take up residence in low-cost motels
in the first place. So, it's time to shine a light on the ignored aftermath of the economic crash and housing crisis which thousands of US citizens are still dealing with
day to day, and, in this case, right on Disney's doorstep.[38]

Baker indicates a hope that audiences will be so moved by the
story that it will cause them to seek out additional information
on this important social issue.

There are a host of different characters in the attached
fifty-two-page script that is dated April 20, 2016. The script
reads more like a sketch or extended scriptment than a
full-blown screenplay. It does contain camera movements
and shot scales, elements normally found in a shooting script,
indicating that Baker was already visualizing the film.

There are not only a lot of kids in this version—ten of them
in all—but also a large number of adult characters. The protagonist's name has been changed from Gin to Moonee, and her
mother has become Halley, after Halley's Comet.[39] Moonee's
age is listed as six and Scooty's as five to seven. Scooty has
just moved into the nearby motel, which is not yet named
Futureland but rather the Arabian Nights. In the initial scene
where Moonee and friends spit on Grandma Stacy's car, the
characters have been switched. It is Scooty who is the new
arrival in the nearby hotel rather than Jancey, who is only a
minor character. Moonee bonds with Scooty similarly to how
she bonds with Jancey in the film, by assisting the other kids in
cleaning off Grandma Stacy's car. Another of the kids, named
Joshy, is Ashley's son. He is involved in the fire in the abandoned condos along with Moonee and Scooty.

There is still a romantic plotline in which Moonee's summer project is to get her first kiss. Scooty becomes her intended target. Toward the end of the script, Moonee takes Scooty to what is left of the abandoned amusement park Splendid China, where they look at the moon. This is where Moonee confides to Scooty her desire to fly there and the genesis of her name, "Moonlight." She tells him, "When I was a kid, my mom told me I discovered it. I knew she was makin' it up but I didn't let her know." Scooty responds, "Maybe, one day, we can go together."[40] Moonee succeeds in achieving her goal of kissing Scooty toward the end of the film, on page 48, but it is simply written as an action rather than as a major dramatic moment in the story.

Halley has a serious drug problem in this version, which also contains more overt violence. She brutally beats Ashley in front of the kids and teenagers by the motel's swimming pool. Bobby, who suffers from PTSD, accidentally kills a pedophile, which causes him to be arrested by the cops. This also brings social workers to the motel, presumably to counsel the children. When the social workers see Ashley's swollen and bruised face, they question her about being in an abusive relationship. She accuses Halley of exposing the children to prostitution. The social workers initially refuse to take any action, but when they take a second look at Halley's room and observe tinfoil and heroin, they decide that it is necessary to separate Moonee from Halley. When the police arrive to take Moonee away, she manages to break free and flees.

Moonee runs to find Scooty, but he fails to understand the gravity of her situation. Here is how it is described in the script: "Moonee makes it to Scooty's room in one piece. He is not there. When she finds him downstairs, she grabs him and tells him they have to make a run for it. The time has come to escape to the moon and she can get them there. Scooty is confused and doesn't go along with this."[41] Moonee then proceeds to take off alone, causing a six-car crash as she crosses the highway toward Disney World, where she ends up riding the rocket in the amusement park, the Astro Orbiter:

> EXT. ENTRANCE SIGN—SUNSET
> Moonee runs toward the entrance sign of the THEME PARK property.
>
> EXT. THEME PARK ENTRANCE GATES—SUNSET
> Moonee is running toward the big parking lot entrance gate.
>
> EXT. THEME PARK—MAIN STREET—SUNSET
> CLOSE ON: Moonee's feet as they run past hundreds of tourists' legs, park maps on the ground.
>
> Her feet pick up speed. She hops over a spilled MOUSE SHAPED ICE CREAM BAR. Her feet leap out of frame.
>
> EXT. THEME PARK—ASTRO ORBITER—MAGIC HOUR
> CLOSE ON: Moonee taking off on a rocket. Arms up in the air toward the moon above. Her hair blows in the wind.[42]

As *The Florida Project* began to move very quickly toward production, which was scheduled to begin in late June 2016, the screenplay underwent major transformations within a very short period. The brief summary of the April 20 screenplay, included as part of the international pitch, suggests how major characters would be reconfigured and major events altered while locations were being secured and casting was in progress. The scriptment that existed in April is a very rough draft and can be viewed more as a promissory note to financial backers. Baker's method of devising scripts is a process of continual revision.

Baker needed to be immersed in the actual location in order to develop the story more fully. He and Shih-Ching Tsou arrived in Kissimmee on May 1, and Bergoch joined them soon afterward. Tsou explains Baker's process of developing the script: "Well, basically, Sean needs to go to the location. He needs to feel the location. He needs to see the people. He needs to verify his ideas. He wants to verify that everything is closest to the reality."[43] The fact that the transformation to the shooting script took place in such a short period is nothing short of miraculous.

The screenwriters were working on the script right up to the start of production—the shooting script is dated June 27, 2016—which caused anxiety for the financial backers and made things that much more difficult for the large union crew, especially in being able to organize the shooting schedule. Yet the screenplay remained a work in progress that was still subject to change. Although the union crew members were skeptical, Baker's core team of collaborators were not at all concerned because he was an experienced filmmaker who had already shot five previous features. Tsou explains, "I know Sean's working style. I know he doesn't need a full script to make a movie. Like *Tangerine*, we really didn't have a full script."[44]

It was after seeing the anime film *When Marnie Was There* (2015) that Bergoch had the idea to change the basic relationship in *The Florida Project* from childhood romance to friendship by having the main story center on the relationship between two young girls: Moonee and Jancey. Baker's previous two films, *Starlet* and *Tangerine*, had centered on female relationships, so the new film would focus on two female relationships: Moonee's relationships with Halley and with Jancey. In the intervening two-month period between drafts of the screenplay, the idea of making the friendship between Moonee and Jancey more central was worked into the story. It would be Jancey who would move into the nearby motel—not the Arabian Nights Hotel, but the Futureland Motel. In actuality, this was the Paradise Motel, which would be transformed by art direction into Futureland.

In the shooting script dated June 27, which is ninety-seven pages in length, the name of the character of Moonee's mother is still spelled "Haley" rather than "Halley," as it will be in the film. Despite the fact that the child actors were already cast and Christopher Rivera was eight at the time, Moonee and Scooty are both listed as six years old. Dicky is listed as three to five years old, but Aiden Malik, the actor who plays him, was also older. Jancey is five, which is accurate, but she has two siblings rather than one, Luci. The opening music was going to be "Bells"—the music of *The Little Rascals*—by the Beau Hunks, not "Celebration." The scene involving the swimsuit selfies comes much earlier in the script.

There is another significant character named Kenn, who works in the laundry room of the Magic Castle and appears to be Bobby's brother. In the script, he is humiliated by another character, Rufus, and eventually by Moonee. There is still a kiss, but it's now between Moonee and Jancey; it is not romantic in this case, but more of an innocent childhood experiment. Halley is still heavily into using drugs. She is described as being "on a narcotic" as she parties at the Magic Castle. It is Halley's drug use that causes the DCF (Florida Department of

Children and Families) to separate Moonee from her. Moonee flees the DCF to see Jancey, but, like Scooty in the previous version, Jancey chooses not to go with her, and Moonee flees alone and runs to Disney World, where she rides the Astro Orbiter. The shooting script concludes, "CLOSE ON: Moonee taking off on the spinning rocket ride. Her hair blows in the wind."[45]

There are many significant changes from the shooting script to the final screenplay as a result of Baker's process of continual change and revision, and his steadfast reliance on improvisation throughout production. Baker, in fact, considers the script dated July 31 to be more accurate and closer to his shooting script than what he used at the start of the production. Scenes were constantly being improvised and written and rewritten, entire characters were dropped or switched, character arcs were changed, and dialogue was altered considerably. For purposes of comparison between the final screenplay and the final film, the July 31 version does indeed turn out to be a more accurate representation of the screenwriters' ideas than what immediately preceded the film, which only affirms Baker's unique scripting process.

It would be unusual for most directors to go into production with so many loose ends in the screenplay, including key scenes, significant characters, and the ending. I think it is fair to say that Baker finds the film he's making in the process of actually shooting it. Kathryn Millard cites the novelist Nelson Algren and the Hong Kong film director Wong Kar-wai as working in a similar "fluid improvisational" manner. According to Millard, Wong has a rough outline of the story, locations, and actors, then simply starts shooting the film.[46] In some ways, that might sound like a fly-by-the seat-of-your-pants approach to filmmaking, but this does not seem to be the case. Baker has a lot of ideas—a number of possible options—yet he hasn't necessarily committed them to paper. He uses what could be considered placeholders instead, then often postpones making a final decision until he finds himself in the actual situation. For Baker, too much preplanning appears to close the door to unforeseen or unanticipated creative possibilities.

COLLABORATION ON THE SCREENPLAY

Although indie cinema tends to be an auteurist cinema, Baker is one of the most collaborative contemporary American filmmakers despite the fact that he often wears many different hats—those of writer, producer, director, cinematographer, and editor—on each production. Most indie directors, for instance, write their own screenplays. This allows them to maintain greater artistic control over the project than is possible within the studio system. When indie directors do collaborate, they seldom work consistently with one screenwriter.

There are a couple of notable examples of a collaboration between an indie filmmaker and a screenwriter. Kelly Reichardt has collaborated with the fiction writer Jon Raymond on five films: *Old Joy* (2006), *Wendy and Lucy* (2008), *Meek's Cutoff* (2010), *Night Moves* (2013), and *First Cow* (2020). Another would be the collaboration between Ronald Bronstein and the Safdie brothers in writing *Heaven Knows What*, *Good Time*, and *Uncut Gems*. In her book *Creative Collaboration*, Vera John-Steiner discusses the emotional issues that factor into such a creative partnership. She writes, "These include care and conflict, fusion and separation, trust, individual artistic identity, and partners' negotiations about the ownership of ideas."[47]

Because cinema is at once a narrative and a visual art, a skillful writer and a gifted director ought to be able to merge their talents. Although Kelly Reichardt and Jon Raymond develop their screenplays together, their roles remain somewhat traditionally defined. Raymond views himself primarily as a fiction writer and is not usually on set once the actual production begins. His contribution is clearly in developing the story—locations, characterization, and dialogue.

Reichardt and Raymond's collaboration represents an instance of what John-Steiner calls "complementary" collaboration. In the complementary mode of collaboration, "differences in training, skill, and temperament support a joint outcome through division of labor."[48] The unique skills of each of the participants are fully engaged in key parts of the artistic process, and those parts blend smoothly in the final work. Alternatively, in "integrative" collaboration, according to John-Steiner, the participants suspend differences to create a common, unitary vision. An example is the birth of Cubism under the auspices of Picasso and Braque, two otherwise very different artists.

The collaboration between Sean Baker and Chris Bergoch on *The Florida Project* is harder to pin down. The two, who have been friends since attending NYU together, have very different sensibilities. Baker's love of art cinema causes him to be less enamored with classical Hollywood narration. As a consequence, he is less concerned with conventional act structure. In *The Florida Project*, for example, Baker was more interested in portraying the world of the kids than he was in having a tight dramatic plot. As a screenwriter who has more mainstream ambitions, Bergoch takes a more traditional approach. About the act structure of the film, Bergoch observes, "It's the core crazy dynamic of Sean and Chris. I can't even believe that it works. It's me on one corner trying to have as much structure as possible, and him on the other corner trying to have zero structure."[49]

Upon seeing *The Florida Project* at the film's premiere at Cannes, noted critic Amy Taubin, who claimed to love the film, worried what effect the film's lack of structure might have on potential audiences. In an interview with Baker, she observes, "There's so little narrative structure that it almost seems like an experimental film. It just has the energy of these kids running wild and this impressionistic portrait of Moonee and Halley fighting for their existence. There isn't a three-act structure or the usual character arcs."[50] In response, Baker claims that he worried that his previous films might be "too narrative heavy."[51] It is true that a number of them rely on traditional narrative devices, such as "ticking clocks." And the last two, cowritten with Bergoch, exhibit more narrative structure. In the same interview, Baker expresses a certain frustration with the conventional expectations of a three-act structure and character arcs, and for the audience "to know what's going on in the first 30 seconds."[52]

Baker took screenwriting courses as a student at NYU and claims to be at least "slightly familiar" with the approach of manual writers like Syd Field.[53] Yet he has strong feelings about the role of structure in a screenplay. Whereas for Field, Linda Seger, and Robert McKee structure is everything—the basis of screenwriting—Baker tends to downplay its importance. In a talk he gave on the subject of screenwriting at BAFTA (the British Academy for Film and Television Arts), Baker told the attendees, "I try not to focus on the forms of structure when writing. I actually never want structure to be apparent.... The minute that I recognize structure, it takes me out. I want to feel like I'm living and breathing with the characters and spending time with them, at least in my films."[54] Although some of his films undoubtedly have a three-act structure, he emphatically states, "I want the acts to be difficult to point out, to find—for the act breaks to be blurred as much as possible."[55]

The way Chris Bergoch approaches the first hour of *The Florida Project*, which is nearly bereft of plot, is almost strictly in terms of character. Baker's co-screenwriter says, "That's why it's a great collaboration, because we each see each other's point of view. And I ultimately will always tell him, 'You're the director; it's your film and we'll do what you want to do,' but he allows me to question things."[56] Bergoch has tried to collaborate with other friends in writing screenplays at various times in his career, but he claims it never worked because he felt there wasn't enough respect for differing points of view.

When asked what makes his collaboration with Baker so successful, Bergoch explains, "Open-mindedness, a willingness to just listen and click into the other person's point of view, even if you're convinced in your brain that there's no way you like this. Just because you never know if you're perceiving it wrong, and you have to take that tunnel vision off and just listen."[57] He adds, "The difference with Sean is that we'll always hear each other out. It's not being married to anything."[58] It's also clear that Bergoch has tremendous respect and admiration for Baker as an artist, emphasizing the fact that he "earned [his] trust years ago."[59]

Although Baker and Bergoch have very different sensibilities, they share certain commonalities: a respect for the critical importance of research, a concern for how place can shape story, and the priority of creating interesting characters over the mechanics of plot. Bergoch explains,

> You hear that story is the most important, but I think Sean and I do agree that we disagree with that, and we think character is the most important and that we would rather spend time with characters that we want to spend time with—with zero story—rather than this great, great story with characters that we just hate and don't care about . . . So we feel like character is the most important, and I think that's the place that is very common ground. Character is greater than story for us.[60]

As with all successful collaborations, Bergoch believes that the final result of their efforts in writing screenplays together is "what neither of [them] would do separately."[61]

Their roles as co-screenwriters are much more complicated because Bergoch not only participated in the writing and preproduction of *The Florida Project* but, as a producer on the project, remained active during the production itself. In fact, Baker wants his co-screenwriter to be on set because for him, screenwriting is a process of scripting that occurs in three stages: writing the script, directing the film, and editing it in postproduction. Through the various stages, the script remains in flux as ideas are revised and new ones discovered.

Because Bergoch is a huge fan of Disney World and has been going to the theme park since he was a young child, he was already very familiar with possible locations for shooting *The Florida Project*. He had even stayed at the Magic Castle previously. As a result, Bergoch played a much greater role in the final film than a traditional co-screenwriter.

Baker and Bergoch take an ethnographic approach when it comes to writing a script. They each consider in-depth research beforehand to be essential. For *The Florida Project*, Baker received a development grant from the nonprofit organization Cinereach, which allowed him to immerse himself in the subject, scout locations, and do some casting. The New York City–based Cinereach has provided funding for a number of important American indie films, including *Beasts of the Southern Wild*, *Beach Rats*, Sandy Tan's *Shirkers* (2018), Tayarisha Poe's *Selah and the Spades* (2019), Kitty Green's *The Assistant* (2019), and Eliza Hittman's *Never Rarely Sometimes Always* (2020).

Baker originally wanted to have a ragtag band of ten kids appear at the beginning of the film and a dog.[62] One of the biggest changes from the screenplay in terms of casting had to do with a change in the children's ages. In researching the film, Baker met a homeless family with three children whose ages were five, six, and eight. The eight-year-old girl was already very aware of her plight. He explains,

I saw a difference, an awareness of surroundings and environment and situation, but I saw it kicking in at eight or nine years old where they were aware of their situation. And the older daughter had a very different demeanor . . . and I guess that was what informed us to stay young because it basically would have been a movie about a frowning girl for most of the two hours.[63]

By chance, Baker had served on the jury of the Indian Film Festival of Los Angeles in 2015. Only one of the films in competition, which were mostly about children, took an approach similar to that of *The Florida Project*, M. Manikandan's

The Crow's Egg (2015). According to Baker, "They kept it light, and the children had that sense of innocence, that sense of wonder and awe that we were looking for with our children."[64]

Because Baker wanted *The Florida Project* to be like *The Little Rascals*, he decided that he probably needed to cast younger children who still retained a sense of childhood innocence. For one thing, it could be funnier if the kids were younger, especially when they use foul language whose meaning they barely understand, such as when they talk sassy to the adults or become excited at the sight of Gloria's naked "boobies." Something like prostitution would not be easily comprehended by younger children, so casting them would help to open up greater possibilities—if Baker could only find the right child actors.

As might be expected, Baker and Bergoch differ in terms of their approach to individual scenes and dialogue. Baker sees a scripted scene as merely a launching pad or a guide. He observes,

> That's the difference between Chris and me. Chris has very specific dialogue that sometimes he's precious about. I am not. This was simply something that could just allow the children to begin talking about the subject—subjects that children talk about. You can see that the stuff that was very scripted for the children didn't make it into the final cut. Most of the time the dialogue that would work with the children was the stuff that I would allow them to be free and just talk about a subject.[65]

According to Baker, the biggest example of this occurs in the short scene of Moonee and Jancey on the seesaw after Halley vomits.

There was dialogue in the script, but it wasn't working, and Baker felt they were wasting a lot of film. In exasperation, he told Prince and Cotto to talk about going back to school, and what that was going to be like for them: "Because the children were going to go back to school in real life, they had something to talk about. And then they started to talk about recess and playing, and there was that really funny moment when Brooklynn, who somehow thought that recess is not cool, suddenly in a bit of improv, exclaims, 'It's just recess. Nothing else!'"[66] Baker explains, "You know that was totally me allowing her to be her in that moment and giving the subject to talk about instead of dogmatically sticking to the script all the time. That was like the nail in the coffin for me in terms of ever having my actors learn dialogue again, especially children."[67]

The production could not afford a proper EPK (electronic press kit), so Alex Coco shot over twenty hours of behind-the-scenes footage of the production, using whatever camera happened to be available. This became the featurette *Under the Rainbow*, which is included in the bonus features of the DVD and Blu-ray. In it, we hear Baker tell the kids—Prince, Cotto, and Rivera—as they eat ice cream in the scene at the Twistee Treat, "Guys, talk about whatever you want. It doesn't have to be the lines."[68] Ken Loach also rails against having actors slavishly stick to the script, as it inhibits authenticity. He believes that it's not what appears on the page that is important, but what ends up on the screen. He remarks, "The page doesn't exist when you see the film, so why adhere to this mannered, formalized thing when simply by rephrasing something you can provoke a response in your actors that is absolutely instinctive and, therefore, true?"[69]

Baker indicates that all actors are different, so it really depends on their particular method. Some actors enjoy learning the lines that are written in the screenplay and shy away from improvising, but he finds that it's a different case with child actors, first-time actors, and nonprofessionals. He has come to realize that having them adhere to the lines in the script is often not very productive. In *The Florida Project*, Baker found that it proved to be a waste of time, which became a precious commodity given the difficult circumstances of the production.

Baker argues that sometimes scripted lines simply don't work on set, no matter how good the performer. He felt that way about a final line in the second scene between Bobby and his son, Jack. In the screenplay, the scene where they move the ice machine ends with Bobby telling Jack about his ex-wife, "And tell her I did not wish her anything. We're all out of wishes over here." Baker was not crazy about the dialogue, but both Bergoch and Dafoe liked the lines, so they shot it that way. Baker thought the line about "wishes" was too much of a Disney reference and regretted not shooting a take without it. As a result, he ended up cutting the line in the editing room.

Baker claims that he is trying not to be "precious" or "dogmatic" about the words in the screenplay. He insists, "I will always tell my actors from this point on that they do not have to learn the script by heart unless they feel they have to for their particular method."[70] He adds a further corollary that if a line feels too scripted while shooting, he will be sure to do a take without it. Since *Tangerine*, provided that he has enough time on set, he's been trying to have the actors perform an action without the dialogue. This represents an attempt to be less reliant on the dialogue within a scene.

The final version of the screenplay wound up being ninety-nine pages, which is very short for a film that would end up having an official running time of one hour and fifty-five minutes. The screenplay is somewhat shorter than a typical script because Baker was intent on creating enough "breathing space" to allow for scenes that were slices of life or incidents, as opposed to a strictly plot-oriented narrative. The film spends a great deal of time observing the kids as they simply hang out together and have summer fun.

I have argued elsewhere that a more minimal script can provide advantages for indie filmmakers, especially those more prone to use improvisation and visual storytelling.[71] It allows the director more flexibility to come up with last-minute ideas or changes, and to take advantage of what might actually be occurring when a scene is being filmed. Chris Bergoch admits, "Sometimes it takes you right up until the moment of actually seeing it unfold live for us to really understand that something could be better."[72] As a result, even though he is working from a screenplay, Baker tends to remain open while he's shooting a scene, so that the writing continues into the process of filming. Bergoch explains, "I think that's why re-shoots happen a lot. People get too married to the material. We're kind of reshooting as we're shooting."[73]

FINANCING AND CASTING THE FILM

Although everyone understands the role of a director or an editor, the role of a producer on a film is much harder to define. The role varies quite a bit, not just on major Hollywood productions but especially on independent films. Some producer credits are honorary titles or a result of some sort of financial arrangement. Some producers work behind the scenes and deal strictly with financial matters, while others are actively engaged during the various phases of production. Shih-Ching

Tsou, for instance, functioned as one of the producers on *The Florida Project*. A longtime and trusted member of the Baker team who codirected *Take Out*, she was more involved with other aspects of this film, such as script development and casting, than with its financing.

Kevin Chinoy and Francesca Silvestri of Freestyle Picture Company had served as producers on *Starlet* and as coproducers on *Tangerine*, which brought recognition to Baker within the film industry. After the critical success of *Tangerine* following its premiere at Sundance in January 2015, there was suddenly renewed interest in *The Florida Project*, the project that Baker had been unable to get off the ground years earlier. Chinoy knew Caroline Kaplan, formerly of IFC Films, who had recently joined Cinereach as the head of creative initiatives. Chinoy and Silvestri arranged for Baker to receive a development grant of $40,000 from Cinereach to do preproduction on *The Florida Project*, which was administered through Freestyle Picture Company. The grant process wound up taking a number of months. Although the team learned informally that the grant would be forthcoming in August, the official email notification from Cinereach came on October 26, 2015.[74] The grant allowed Baker and his co-screenwriter, Bergoch, to take numerous research trips to Orlando in order to develop the story.

Chinoy and Silvestri were in serious discussions about potential financiers for *The Florida Project* at the Sundance Film Festival in January 2016. June Pictures, a Los Angeles–based production company, was considered a strong possibility. Alex Saks had worked as an agent for ICM Partners before leaving to serve as the president of June Pictures, which was newly created with financier Andrew Duncan to produce feature films and documentaries. About making a deal with June Pictures, Chinoy explains, "We didn't actually connect in person at Sundance but immediately during the month of February were working on a potential agreement between us. We met soon thereafter and started looking at an agreement right after that. We met with them on February 29 and agreed to move forward together in principle at that time."[75]

At that late February meeting, which included Baker, the general budget range of the film was agreed upon. Baker and the producers did not have a completed screenplay to pitch—only a rough treatment for the film. They had hired a line producer in Florida, Elayne Schneiderman Schmidt, to help them put together a budget based on crew and how Baker had conceived of the film. Schmidt wound up with the titles of line producer and executive producer in the final credits. According to Chinoy, "On March 17, I sent Alex Saks a detailed budget, production calendar and other materials.... We worked together over the next number of weeks to continue to revise and shape as the project became further defined creatively, but that process frankly went on throughout all of prep and even into production."[76]

Although there still was not a completed screenplay for the film, June Pictures agreed to provide Baker with a budget that eventually reached $3.6 million to make *The Florida Project*, considerably larger than the miniscule amount with which he had made his previous feature, *Tangerine*. The film was only the second project for June Pictures. The company's agreement to finance the film involved something of a risk, especially because the film did not have any big-name stars attached at the time. Yet Chinoy and Silvestri and June Pictures believed in Baker's talent, even if his modus operandi of making films was radically unconventional by industry standards. As Chinoy explains, "As a producer, Sean makes the job easy for all the right reasons, and makes it impossibly hard for all the right reasons."[77]

Baker, however, made an unexpected detour between feature projects. He was asked by Humberto Leon and Carol Lim, the creative designers of the French clothing line Kenzo, to make a promotional film featuring their 2016 spring collection. Baker was given carte blanche to make a short film for the LVMH fashion company. At the time they contacted him (as a result of *Tangerine*), Baker only had a location in mind for a project, Slab City, but that was all. Slab City is a former military base in the Sonoran Desert about an hour's drive from the Mexican border. By chance, the location was already an inspiration to the designers of the new collection—they had a photo of it on their desk—so Baker decided to accept the assignment. Baker turned the project into a short film entitled *Snowbird* (2016), which used a mix of local residents and professional actors and wound up being eleven minutes long.

Snowbird had important ramifications for Baker's next feature. One of the most significant was that he hired Alexis Zabé, who had shot Carlos Reygadas's *Silent Light* (2007) and *Post Tenebras Lux* (2012), to be the director of photography. Zabé has an exceptional eye for composition, which is evident from the wide landscapes he shot using an iPhone 6s. According to his coworkers on the project, Zabé also has a very laid-back personality. He proved to be a great fit with the Baker team, which included Chris Bergoch, Darren Dean, and Shih-Ching Tsou.

Speaking about Baker and the project, Stephonik Youth explains, "I think *Snowbird* was sort of a test. He'd surrounded himself with people that might be on *The Florida Project*. I didn't know at the time, but I sort of passed the test."[78] She served as the production designer and also composed the music for the film. Baker shot in two of the campers on location in Slab City, but Youth's production design skills were put to the test when she had to recreate an additional two campers on a movie ranch right outside Los Angeles, which was more accessible for the professional actors.

Samantha Quan had an associate producer credit, and Alex Coco, a recent MFA grad from USC, was a postproduction assistant on the film. Coco would become an important member of the Baker crew for the next film by serving as the assistant to the director; shooting the behind-the-scenes featurette *Under the Rainbow*, about the making of *The Florida Project*; and serving as the postproduction coordinator. Given that he would be working on a much larger scale, Baker clearly understood that his next feature would be far more challenging than anything he had done previously. His strategy was to surround himself with battle-tested collaborators who shared a similar vision.

The shooting of *Snowbird* for Kenzo served as an important trial run for *The Florida Project*, but the editing and postproduction of the film wound up taking much longer than Baker had anticipated. The film was officially released on February 3, 2016, and Baker also had responsibilities to promote it through interviews and appearances. At the same time, Baker was under intense pressure from the producers to be working on the new feature. *The Florida Project* could only be shot in the summer due to having child actors in major roles. *Snowbird* put him very behind schedule on the new project, especially in terms of being able to complete the final draft

of the screenplay, secure locations, and deal with the enormously difficult challenges of casting.

Casting is a crucial part of the development of the screen
idea. As Chris Bergoch puts it, "Sean and I like to say that we
draw a picture and then we all color it in with the actors."[79]
The use of nonprofessional actors, or "first-time actors," the
term Baker prefers, has become commonplace in indie cinema in the new century. A number of factors account for this,
including the advent of digital technology, which allows filmmakers to shoot their films more cheaply. Filmmakers from
Gus Van Sant to the mumblecore filmmakers—Andrew Bujalski, Joe Swanberg, and Aaron Katz—have used first-time
actors to create a greater sense of realism.

Baker's use of first-time actors, however, is particularly
notable within indie cinema. The prevalence of cell phones and
social media have turned the average person into a performer.
Baker indicates, however, that not everyone has the ability to
perform in a film. They need to have a certain skill set, but
if they have that, then for a director it becomes "about creating a casual environment where they [the performers] are
comfortable and having fun."[80]

Baker resisted the temptation to cast a well-known female
star in the role of Halley, the financially strapped mother of
Moonee. Britney Spears was one of the names discussed, but
Baker worried about the incongruity of a famous star playing
such a down-and-out character. Samantha Lay has argued
that social realist films generally avoid casting internationally
famous stars because it "would undermine the film's ability
to focus on the social conditions and milieu they evoke." Lay
adds, "Imagine how different Ken Loach's *My Name Is Joe*
(1998) would be with Tom Cruise perfecting a Scots accent

and how the focus would shift away from social issues onto the angst-ridden performance of a major Hollywood star looking for an Oscar nomination."[81]

Baker instead cast a first-time performer, Bria Vinaite, based on the Instagram videos of her that he found online, using social media to broaden the scope of his casting. Vinaite emigrated from Lithuania to the United States at an early age and grew up in Bay Ridge, Brooklyn. Baker used some of the remaining money from Cinereach to bring Vinaite down for a short audition with the child actors. They created a reel of her interacting with the kids to present to the financiers, who supported Baker's decision to cast her in the role of Halley. From a business standpoint, it probably was a risky decision, but, according to Chinoy, the financiers were really making a bet on Sean Baker.[82]

Baker first discovered Mela Murder, a choreographer and dancer from Brooklyn, in a short film by Clayton Vomero entitled *Gang* (2015), which played on the "Dazed and Confused" platform on Vimeo. In fact, he wrote the part of Ashley with her specifically in mind. Baker, however, was initially informed that the actor was unavailable. As a result, Baker began to look at other actors for the role of Ashley. When he wasn't successful at finding anyone who he felt fit the part better, he decided to reach out to Mela Murder directly. In doing so, he learned that she was not only available but also very interested in playing the part. Baker knew of Sandy Kane, a Times Square street performer known for exposing herself in public, and got the idea that she would make a colorful resident of the Magic Castle. She was likewise excited to be in the film.

Baker always planned to cast a more well-known actor in the role of Bobby. Through the casting agent, Carmen Cuba,

word had spread that *The Florida Project* was seeking an established actor for the role. As a result, the production began
to receive inquiries from agents. There were a number of
intriguing possibilities, including Willem Dafoe, but the start
of production was also imminent. Kevin Chinoy explains:

> We were looking for options at the time. Frank Frattaroli,
> Willem's manager and a long-time friend of Francesca's
> [Silvestri], knew of the project and communicated that
> Willem was a fan of Sean's past work and was interested.
> We arranged for Sean to fly up to NY from Orlando
> during formal prep for a day, just to go have dinner with
> Willem. The meeting went well and he was cast! Again,
> closing a deal with lawyers and agents takes time and we
> were moving forward with him and even shooting before
> the deal was formally closed.[83]

Baker flew to New York City to meet with Dafoe on June 17,
which indicates just how close this meeting was to the start of
production. Although Baker initially worried that Dafoe might
be too big a star, it was impossible for him to pass up an opportunity to cast an actor of such high caliber. In addition,
having a major name attached to the film helped to reassure
the financial backers of the project. Baker was a friend of the
actor Macon Blair and always planned to use him in some way
in the film. The decision to cast him had been made on May
11, nearly five weeks earlier.

In casting the children, Baker employed an open approach.
He was more interested in finding the right kids than in fitting
them into specific roles. In the casting sessions, some children
were excellent at delivering lines but became totally lost when

suddenly asked to improvise a scene. One of the improv exercises used in the casting sessions involved a situation where it was the younger kids' turn to use the swimming pool and they needed to kick out a bunch of teenagers who were still occupying it. Many of the young kids in the auditions did not know how to respond to the situation, and simply froze.

Given his interest in social realism, Baker's initial goal was to recruit kids who lived in the motels as actors. The film's line producer, Elayne Schneiderman Schmidt, contacted Jennifer Conrader, the owner of CROWDshot, and Mark Mullen and Associates to do the Florida casting or location casting, as opposed to principal casting, which was done out of Los Angeles by Carmen Cuba. CROWDshot's first charge was to assist the production team in attempting to cast kids who lived in the motels for the principal roles. Baker gave the casting agency certain leads based on the research that he and Bergoch had conducted on the homeless kids who lived in the motels. Conrader and her casting coordinator, Patti Wiley, began the process by following up on the leads. They also canvassed the homeless motels along Highway 192 and put up flyers. They arranged to hold two different casting sessions in the motels, as well as at the Community Hope Center in Kissimmee, hoping to find kids who would fit the bill.

When Conrader and Wiley initially read the scriptment for the film, it particularly resonated with Wiley, who saw a reflection of herself in the film. Raised by a single mom, Wiley had grown up in motels in Tampa and in Michigan. She had just been through the traumatic experience of losing her longtime partner the previous December. When she met Baker and he explained why he wanted to make the film, she immediately felt a strong kinship with what he was attempting to do, and she set out to help him. While street casting in the motels, she saw Christopher Rivera, whom she refers to as "CJ," "riding down the railing" outside the Paradise Motel. As Wiley spoke to him, his mother came out, and Wiley found herself surrounded by a bunch of other kids. Based on her interactions, Wiley thought that Rivera "really stood out" and had "a spark about him."[84] She shot video of Rivera and the other kids, which she sent to Baker, who was impressed. Finding other kids, however, proved not to be an easy task.

Baker used street casting to locate another possible performer for one of the major roles. By sheer coincidence, he spotted the redheaded Valeria Cotto at a local Target store when he went there on an errand one evening. Baker gave Cotto's mother, Ivelisse Rijos, his business card, and she eventually turned up at a casting session with her daughter. Baker really wanted to cast Cotto, but her age proved to be an obstacle. She was only five years old at the time, which meant that the length of the daily shoots would have to be curtailed considerably due to strict child labor laws on films. If he cast her, they would have to reduce the shoot time by two hours each day.

As the start of production drew closer, it became obvious that the search for child actors needed to be widened. Although Baker did not want to cast in Los Angeles, Shih-Ching Tsou contacted casting agencies and began to look at other child actors. The biggest challenge was finding someone to play the central role of Moonee. Despite the necessity of having to expand the search, Baker remained adamant about casting actual Florida kids in the various roles. Baker's expanded search, however, allowed Conrader and Wiley to access CROWDshot's considerable talent base. That's how Baker was able to find Aiden Malik to play Dicky.

Yet, despite having a casting director and holding numerous local casting calls and auditions, Baker was still unable to turn up any child actors who fit the lead role. As Baker has indicated in numerous subsequent interviews, he was looking for the equivalent of Spanky McFarland of *The Little Rascals*, one of the main inspirations behind the film. As the start of production drew nearer, Baker was beginning to become desperate. Patti Wiley felt as frustrated as Baker. She grasped that the situation had become so dire that Baker was contemplating postponing the film if he couldn't find the right child actor to play Moonee.

Late one night, Wiley sat at her computer, going through the various headshots in her database, when Brooklynn Prince's face suddenly appeared on the screen. From their conversations, Wiley had an idea of what Baker was looking for, and Prince seemed to have that special quality. Wiley recounts, "She looked like the vision he had given . . . to me; it was like a miracle."[85] She immediately texted Baker about her discovery. Wiley and Baker contacted Prince's mother to have her come in for an audition. Courtney Prince brought the six-year-old Brooklynn to an open casting call that was held at the Magnuson Hotel in Kissimmee. She was one of four child actors that CROWDshot had selected from their talent base to audition for the part of Moonee.

When Prince interacted with Christopher Rivera and Valeria Cotto, the chemistry among them was unmistakable to everyone there. The three kids immediately bonded. According to Wiley, "When those kids got together, it was magic."[86] Rivera, for instance, began to do push-ups, while Prince responded by doing squats; the two kids doing calisthenic exercises struck Baker as an extremely comic image. It didn't take long for him to become convinced that he had finally found his much sought-after lead actor. Not only did Prince have previous acting experience—her mother is an acting coach—but she exhibited exceptional talent for such a young child actor. Baker, in fact, considers Prince to be a prodigy. Samantha Quan, who became the film's acting coach, calls her "the youngest Method actor I have ever met in my life."[87] Kevin Chinoy, the film's producer, is convinced that Prince is destined to become a major star.[88]

Prince's parents were a bit apprehensive, especially about the foul language contained in the script, but Baker and their daughter, who really wanted to be cast in the film, convinced them that it was simply a fictional role that wouldn't carry over into her actual life. The main trick in casting the child actors was that they had to be able to memorize the written lines in the script but also be able to make the words their own. Baker was asking the child actors to be able to improvise as well, and often in a comedic way.

Baker wanted to cast Valeria Cotto, but he was under pressure from the producers to try to find someone a year older. Yet once Brooklynn Prince was cast as Moonee, Baker decided that Cotto was worth the even greater restrictions that casting her would impose upon their already tight production schedule. Compounding the issue was the fact that Baker had lobbied to have a sixty-day shoot but the budget only allowed for thirty-five days, which the director felt was much too rushed. Baker believed that Cotto provided a strong physical and emotional contrast to Prince. He considered this to be of critical importance because the friendship between Moonee and Jancey had by that time become such a central part of the story.

Although Baker felt uncomfortable casting an A-list actor for the role of a beleaguered homeless mother, Halley, casting a first-time performer to play opposite someone of the stature of Dafoe represented a big gamble on the director's part. Yet, with the help of Samantha Quan, Bria Vinaite learned how to create a range of possibilities for her role. Circumstances led Quan to become the acting coach on the film. She proved invaluable in terms of working with the child actors as well as with Vinaite and Mela Murder.

Quan, who grew up in Vancouver, has an advanced degree in acting from New York University. Peggy Lewis, a close family friend, had an acting school, PierStudios, in Manhattan, where Quan learned mask work and the methods of Jacques Lecoq and Jerzy Grotowski. While in graduate school, she assisted Lewis in teaching acting classes to adults and kids. After she graduated in 2001, Quan moved to Los Angeles, where she worked as an actor in television. Influenced by her work with Lewis, she also offered private coaching on the side. Quan was often hired as an acting coach to work with first-time performers, who are typically cast by directors on the basis of their authenticity for a particular part.

After seeing Yoon Je-kyoon's *Miracle on 1st Street* (2007), Baker was impressed with the film's use of long and uninterrupted takes of children who had the ability to seem natural and also emote. He wanted to do something similar on *The Florida Project*. The director, however, had no prior experience working with children. Quan indicated that in order for him to be able to replicate what he admired so much about the Korean film, he would need to learn how to work with kids. When Baker asked her for help, Quan agreed to work with the child actors. After Baker cast two inexperienced actors, Bria Vinaite and Mela Murder, in major roles, it quickly became obvious to the director that they would also benefit from coaching. This led to Quan serving as acting coach for them as well. In fact, she wound up working with them not only in preparation for the production but also during the production itself.

Quan contends that working with children and first-time actors is not all that different, because "at the end of the day what you want is a performance that doesn't feel like a performance."[89] She explains,

> What you want is for everyone to feel comfortable "being," and letting them be themselves because that's why they were hired. . . . Sean chooses people a lot of the time based on a look and a feeling and a vibe that they give, so if that's what he wants, the goal is to try and get them to the point that they feel like they're not acting.[90]

Her goal was for them to exist in that moment as a character and for the audience not to be aware of them trying to act. Quan sees the role of acting coach as a position of trust because it helps to give the actors a greater sense of security.

In a sense, it could be argued that Vinaite was already a performer on Instagram. Quan, however, believes that there is a difference between performing on social media, such as YouTube or Instagram, and acting in a film such as *The Florida Project*, in which the overriding aesthetic is social realism. Quan observes, "The idea [in the film] is to feel like you are watching people in their real lives, while performance on social media is much more presentational and aware of the camera."[91] With Instagram, the person is often thinking about determining the best angle of self-presentation—after all, it's about taking pictures of yourself—whereas acting in film requires the person to forget about the camera completely. The goal of acting in a film is precisely the opposite of that of social media—instead of "posing," it's about trying not to pose. Part of the preparation for the film was getting the first-timers to "play" in a manner similar to that of the kids.

Quan set up the equivalent of an acting boot camp for the child actors: Brooklynn Prince, Valeria Cotto, Christopher Rivera, and Aiden Malik. The most important purpose of the acting classes was getting the kids to bond with each other. Indeed, Prince and Cotto became fast friends. Quan devised a number of acting games for them. As an example, they would become certain animals based on names drawn from a hat. Other animals might become friends or enemies who had a piece of candy the person desired. She created alternative situations that mirrored scenes in the film but were not the exact scenes. As a result, the child actors were fresh, but still prepared, when it came time to shoot the actual scene. Early in *The Florida Project*, Moonee and Scooty give Jancey a tour of the different rooms and the residents in the Magic Castle motel. In the workshop, Quan created a parallel situation: she had them create various art objects that were then placed in a museum. The child actors then acted as docents, explaining each art work, who made it, and why.

One of the ideas in *The Florida Project* is that the motels serve as a parallel universe to nearby Disney World. Despite the grim conditions, for the children, this is nevertheless their kingdom. According to Quan, "In moments they feel like kings and queens of this place."[92] There are many shots of the children walking in the film. For them, the act of walking—their small bodies moving freely through space—appears to be a fun experience. Quan did walking exercises with them. She had the children walk as if they were trekking through mud, as if they were swimming, as if they had just heard the saddest news, as if no one could tell them what to do, as if they were invisible, as if they were embarrassed, and so forth.

For the tour scene of the Magic Castle by Moonee and Scooty, she developed what she called a "cool kids walk." She explains, "This is the walk that they do when they feel empowered showing Jancey their kingdom. So when we were shooting those scenes and Sean wanted to hold on them walking, I would just say to them, 'Remember you're the cool kids, so put it in your bodies,' and they knew what I meant."[93] For the child actors, ownership often somehow translated into dancing. Quan observes, "It was as if they would hear music in their head and walk accordingly."[94] In the film, the dancing spilled into other scenes.

Bria Vinaite also participated in the sessions with the children. During the workshop, Quan created exercises with the children and Vinaite in order for them to bond and become a unit. She used improv games to build upon the relationships. In one involving Prince and Vinaite, they took turns playing a shop owner watching a customer who may not have money. Quan made up various games and exercises to encourage the actors to become more playful. According to Quan, the last thing you want first-time actors to do is to rehearse over and over.[95]

Quan worked with Vinaite and Murder each night and before their scenes. This involved going over lines and actions, and consisted of a combination of improv work and scene work. Because the film was being shot out of sequence, Quan created a physical and emotional map of Vinaite's character

Bria Vinaite with acting coach Samantha Quan. Photo courtesy of Marc Schmidt.

for the actor. If something was missing or if there was a "hole" in terms of the characterization, Quan used the workshops to figure out how to get the actors out of themselves. In the case of Vinaite, this often involved getting her to change the action or tactic so it wouldn't become stagnant. For instance, instead of getting angry over a particular situation, such as not being able to find a job, Quan would have Vinaite make her laugh or feel some other emotion. The idea was to get Vinaite to vary her reactions so there was never a single objective. After going through an entire range of different possibilities with a monologue, she would then say to Vinaite, "Now throw it all away, and tell me what you want."[96]

Quan never wanted Vinaite to "overintellectualize what she

was doing because that could kill spontaneity."[97] Quan went through the script line by line with actions and intentions. Prior to that she got Vinaite to figure out an entire character history, based on herself and other things that she could tap into for the role. Quan asked her questions about every single scene. When it came to a certain situation, she never gave Vinaite a single choice or option, but rather multiple possibilities (unless she was instructed by Baker that a scene or situation had to be played in a specific way). Working with Vinaite, her approach was always to talk about a particular scene so that they could figure it out together. Vinaite was already close to the character of Halley, which is why she was cast in the first place. Her physicality—her energy and spirit—already helped to shape her character. If, for some reason, Quan felt that Vinaite was somehow "off" in her approach to a scene, she tried to get her to choose something different so that it would become part of character development.

Despite her intensive acting work with Quan, Vinaite felt a need to stay very close to the script once shooting commenced. As might be expected, having to play opposite an experienced professional actor of the stature of Willem Dafoe became a huge challenge for her. Because Vinaite was extremely nervous, not only did she have to stick to the lines as a kind of security blanket, but Baker initially had to assist her with the line readings, which included giving her the inflections of how certain lines were supposed to be said. Vinaite, however, was gradually able to loosen up and become more confident in herself as the production progressed. According to Baker, "By the second or third week, she became much more comfortable doing her own stuff."[98] He had nothing but praise for her development: "Bria's acting just kept growing. By the time we did this long Steadicam shot—where she slaps that thing on the window—I knew I didn't [have to] worry that I'd have to use editing to manipulate the performance. She completely held this five-minute take with Willem."[99]

Similar to the Safdie brothers, Baker believes that a mixture of professional and first-time actors creates a particular chemistry on set that contributes to the kind of naturalistic performances he is seeking to create in his films. According to Quan, "Professionals have way of working; they know what to do. With first-timers, there's a freshness of energy and a playfulness that can free things up and keep them from being stale. It's about lessening the degree of artifice, so that it's replicating human behavior."[100] On the set of *The Florida Project*, Willem Dafoe's experience rubbed off on the first-time performers, such as Vinaite, Mela Murder, and the child actors, while their freedom and utter lack of a method, in turn, had a positive effect on him.

Speaking about his experience on the set of *The Florida Project* with first-time actors, Dafoe observes, "If you cast well and people are not self-conscious and they're very present— even if they don't have traditional actor skills—you get something else. You get that presence; you get that commitment; you get that kind of freshness."[101] Dafoe claims that helped to keep him very much in the "moment" and "not going to the same impulses all the time." Dafoe admired the fact that Baker was willing to abandon the screenplay whenever necessary in favor of improvisation, especially when a scene wasn't working.

In the bonus feature detailing the production, there is footage of Baker showing Brooklynn Prince how he wants her to perform in a scene. Because Baker was not used to working with child actors, his initial directions to them were much too broad. Quan attempted to get Baker to simplify his directions and be more specific about what he wanted the child actors to do in a particular scene. How they would process more general directions often had unpredictable results, so Baker began to demonstrate the actions they needed to perform. He explains,

> You can't just say, "I want you to walk from here to there and deliver your line." I need you to do this [stands up, walks over to one part of the room] "1, 2, 3, 4, and then say your line." You actually have to do that, but you have to get them comfortable enough where it doesn't look like they have been practicing it, and then I ask them to improvise.[102]

It's clear from the performances of Brooklynn Prince, Valeria Cotto, and Christopher Rivera that over the course of the film Baker became extremely adept at directing child actors.

The Making of
The Florida Project

PREPRODUCTION AND THE CHALLENGES
OF PRODUCTION

Sean Baker initially thought of *The Florida Project* as having muted colors in the vein of Ulrich Seidl's *Import/Export* (2007). Alexis Zabé, his director of photography, argued for warmer and brighter colors for a film that takes place in the Florida sun. Baker realized that Zabé was right. He decided that heightened color and sound would be more appropriate for a film that essentially deals with the experience of childhood. The production designer, Stephonik Youth, strongly agreed with the decision and made it her mission to add bright splashes of color to the sets wherever possible.

After working with the iPhone on *Tangerine*, Baker decided that he wanted to shoot *The Florida Project* on 35 mm film for a combination of reasons. Baker is something of a purist when it comes to film and considers himself to be an advocate for keeping the medium alive. Despite the fact that he has shot digital features, he nevertheless believes digital to be an inferior medium. He thinks that digital images tend to be very "aggressive." In contrast, Baker notes that celluloid film has a "hypnotic" quality that tends to draw the viewer into the image she or he is seeing. With *The Florida Project*, he remarks, "I wanted audiences to feel that subconsciously they were returning to their youth and connecting with these characters, and I think the quality of the image actually lends itself to that."[1] In terms of the decision to shoot 35 mm, he offers a quick summary: "So to break it down, it was to keep the medium alive, it was for archival purposes, but it was also for the sophistication and organic nature of the look."[2] He claims that it also had the side effect of keeping both cast and crew disciplined, including the child actors, because everyone on set became cognizant of the additional expense involved in shooting film.

Zabé has shot a number of features in 35 mm, including two for the noted Mexican director Carlos Reygadas. Due to his strong background in film, he was initially looking forward to shooting a digital feature when Baker approached him to be the DP on *The Florida Project*, before learning that the plan was to shoot it in 35 mm. In contrast to Baker, Zabé believes that there are many subtleties to the digital format, which he often uses when shooting commercials and music videos. For him, it is very much about the difference between a mechanical/chemical medium and an electronic one. In referencing Wayne Wang's use of the digital format in *A Thousand Years of Good Prayers* (2007), Zabé observes, "I was astonished by the stillness of the frame. Digital has a stillness to the frame that you can never get on film. Film always has a bit of a jitter to it. There is mechanical movement there versus digital, in which the frame is just still. And I remember that the stillness of the frame really added to the story."[3]

Zabé notes that "the basic difference between digital and film is that your relationship to the material becomes more of a dialogue versus the kind of pen-pal relationship that you have

with film."[4] He highlights the difference between the imme-
diacy of the digital format—the ability to see the footage right
after shooting it—and having to wait several days to get the
footage back from the lab. He notes that by the time the dailies
come back from the lab, new material has already been shot,
so, in a sense, the film has moved "beyond that." Zabé adds, "So
when you look at those dailies, you're going back in time, so it
is more [of] an epistolary relationship, just like letter writing
in a way, where you put it in an envelope, wait a few days, and
eventually get a response."[5]

In shooting *The Florida Project* on 35 mm film, Zabé used a
Panavision Millennium XL2 camera and E Series Anamorphic
prime lenses (introduced in the 1980s) to shoot the daytime
scenes. Although the Panavision camera is more cumbersome
than an Arriflex, Zabé chose the camera to give him greater
options in terms of the range of lenses available. His basic approach involved "trying to find how the different elements of
reality would fit into our story."[6] This was also true of how
Zabé approached lighting. He explains, "I really like to work
in an uncluttered set. For me, it's very liberating to have the
flexibility and the freedom to keep the creative process alive
even during shooting. We feed off of reality a lot; if you shield
yourself with lighting and cables and trucks, suddenly you can
only catch small glimpses of reality in the gaps that are left."[7]

Zabé used very few lights in shooting the daylight scenes:
a couple of fluorescents and a couple of 1800 watt HMIs. This
allowed him to extend the day when shooting inside the motel
by placing additional lights outside the window to simulate
daylight. Zabé believes that having a lot of lighting equipment
slows down production when the direction of a shot has to
be switched. He explains, "I don't like to light too much in

general. I like to light as little as possible to stay flexible."[8] He
also indicates that there was no real budget for lights on the
production.

For the night scenes, Zabé also wanted flexibility to shoot
with minimum lighting. Tests proved that 35 mm negative had
a "dark quality" that was at odds with the rest of the film, so he
used an Alexa Mini and transferred the digital output to film.
Zabé found that it provided him with a number of advantages,
especially in terms of flexibility:

> Where film can't really be underexposed too much, dig-
> ital works very well underexposed, and it still kept that
> fairy tale, ice-creamy, soft look, even in very low-lit ex-
> teriors, where we only had a couple of sodium lights in
> the parking lot and a couple of old light bulbs lining the
> corridor to the hotel. We decided to do that for the night
> exteriors and that really helped to keep it as loose and as
> free as the day exteriors.[9]

Zabé admits that the tight schedule had the practical effect
of making him use natural light as much as possible, which
also fit the aesthetic of the film. He relied on the production
designer, Stephonik Youth, through subtle touches to the
mise-en-scène and costuming, to create "the color palette
[that] could take it up to that fantastic, more imaginary child's
point-of-view."[10]

Youth has worked as a freelancer in still photography and
music as well as art direction and production design. She
performed multiple tasks on *Prince of Broadway*, handling,
among other things, the production design and costumes, but
it was a microbudget film. Although she had experience as a

production designer on commercials, serving in that capacity on *The Florida Project* was a much bigger and more challenging task. She worked closely with Baker and Zabé in creating the visual aesthetic of the film, as well as in tackling the lighting and wardrobe to determine the color palette within the frame; she wanted it to have the look of a still photograph.

Youth's meticulous, hands-on approach often rankled the union team because she used unorthodox materials or her own ingenuity to achieve some effect—such as using actual crayons to draw on the wall—in ways that are not typically done within the industry. Youth was always going for extreme subtlety and an aesthetic that fit with the realism of the film. The production design team she supervised, however, was more used to working on commercials. She observes, "Everything that I tried to go with as far as my team was concerned would always end up being exaggerated, and I would have to descale it."[11] Youth's skills as a production designer were also needed when it came to choosing the film's major locations.

Baker was conflicted about his choice of locations, especially when it came to the main setting of the film. He loved the idea of the Magic Castle because Moonee could live in an alternate castle. It had recently received a facelift, so the production team would have to "distress" the location in order to make it appear the way it had some years earlier. On the other hand, one of the motels along Highway 192 was downright seedy and rundown, and much more realistic in terms of the kind of environment he wanted to depict. It was extremely dangerous—a center for drug trafficking, prostitution, and gang activity—and reflected the problems that homeless residents faced on a daily basis. Baker's efforts to do research there, however, got him thrown off the property. When Baker had his location manager contact the hotel about using it as a possible site, the owners wanted no part of the film, making his choice easier.

Despite its appropriate name, one drawback of the Magic Castle Inn and Suites was its proximity to the nearby helicopter landing area, which created an enormous amount of continuous noise, but Baker did not consider that to be an insurmountable obstacle. In fact, it became a visual and sonic element that he was able to incorporate into the film. The hotel had recently been painted a very bright purple color as part of a beautification effort in the area, and this seemed serendipitous in terms of how color would be used as an important element of the film. The management of the hotel turned out to be amenable to allowing the production to shoot there. Although the production could not afford to take over such a large motel for the length of time they needed to shoot there, the team was able to rent rooms on adjacent floors that would serve as the motel rooms where Halley and Moonee and Ashley and Scooty resided.

The Paradise Inn was chosen for the location where Jancey and Dicky lived. The motel already had the colorful rockets as part of its main sign, but Youth was tasked with transforming it into the Futureland Motel through her production design. The Paradise Inn was a more rundown hotel than the Magic Castle. The room that served as Grandma Stacy's was occupied by a homeless family. The young girl who played Luci in the film lived in the room, so she wound up being cast as Jancey's younger sister and appears in the scenes that were shot there.

US Highway 192 had undergone a notable transition from when Baker and Bergoch had first thought about shooting the film. Large parts of the highway were fast disappearing, such as Splendid China, which began to be dismantled in 2013 after a period of vandalism and was eventually redeveloped into the Margaritaville Resort Orlando. By the time shooting began, the entire area was undergoing a transformation, so part of the production design involved trying to recreate the way it had looked four years earlier, when Baker and Bergoch first conceived of the idea for the film.

Baker had spent a great deal of time researching the room interiors of the homeless motels. Stephonik Youth's job during production was to create a realistic and consistent look to the various locations, using photos of the rooms of homeless families as a guide. At times that meant distressing the interiors through art direction. Transforming a motel room into a believable home for Halley and Moonee was one of her biggest challenges. It had to look like they actually lived there. Besides the photos she had as a reference and her own ideas, Youth also consulted with Vinaite about the possessions she thought her character might have. Creating a believable space included elements such as Moonee's scribbles on the walls, the clutter in the bathroom and on top of the TV stand, the various clothes that hang from an open rack, a tapestry of a wolf howling at a face in the moon (the outer space theme), Hawaiian lei necklaces on the wall and draped around a lampshade, and numerous stray bottles left wherever.

The exterior of the Magic Castle also took a great deal of detailed work. Bikes and portable coolers had to be strategically placed. Various items were draped over the railings: colorful beach blankets, articles of clothing, bedsheets, and afghans. Youth added garbage and splashes of color to the various locations. In the abandoned condos, a member of the prop team added graffiti to the walls. In *Under the Rainbow*, we

see the name "Alexander" being written, as Bergoch explains
that Alexander and Lampwick are the bad little boys from
Paradise Island in Disney's *Pinocchio* (1940).[12] Glass and po-
tentially toxic materials had to be removed and replaced with
empty cans, bottles, newspapers, plastic bags, old furniture,
and household items, as well as the clusters of white insulation
strewn on the floor that Moonee imagines to be "ghost poop."

On Baker films, key members of the team often shift in
their responsibilities. Before preproduction, Shih-Ching Tsou's
role as producer focused on story development. She provided
notes and feedback on the script ideas and the screenplay as
Baker and Bergoch worked on them. During preproduction,
Tsou scouted locations in Kissimmee and more or less over-
saw the casting of the film. She was tasked with finding the
child actors. Baker and Tsou engaged in "street casting." They
scouted Walmart and Target stores looking for possible actors.

During production, Tsou, who also had a small role in *Tangerine*, acted in the role of the wholesale merchant who sells
Halley the bottles of perfume for resale. She was also mainly
involved in background casting (extras). Although the production hired a local company, CROWDshot, to cast extras, Tsou
worked with them to be sure to get the right people for various
scenes that needed background extras. Drawing on her roots in
guerrilla filmmaking, she also recruited extras whom she happened to spot when the production shot at various locations.

Kevin Chinoy and Francesca Silvestri, on the other hand,
worked closely with the financiers, different agencies, the line
producer, and senior crew members. Their job was to support
Baker in what he wanted to do creatively. "But, at the same
time," Chinoy emphasizes, "we also have a responsibility—from
a fiduciary standpoint—to the people who are putting up the

money."[13] Their main job was to keep the film on budget, as well as deal with the myriad financial issues that developed during the course of production.

One budgetary crisis that developed before the start of production had to do with a tax incentive from the state of Florida. According to Chinoy, "When we were landing the financing, the Florida Tax Incentive got pulled. We were supposed to get more than half a million dollars in a rebate, but the state government didn't renew it."[14] This unexpected development precipitated a crisis in terms of the financing. Already committed to the project financially, June Pictures ended up agreeing to supplement the funds that originally had been expected from the state. But the production nevertheless lost some local crew members when this happened. They took jobs in the burgeoning film industry in nearby Georgia.

This was only one of a number of major calamities that befell *The Florida Project*. At the last minute, immediately before the start of production, a county manager blocked permits for the shooting of the film because he decided that the script presented a rather unflattering picture of Osceola County. As a result, the production team had to readjust the shooting schedule in order to shoot on private property rather than public property while this issue was being resolved. The first scene they shot was at the Twistee Treat, which allowed the production to set up and work in the parking lot.

The blocking of permits nevertheless posed a serious threat to the film. The producers hired lawyers to fight this decision, but it nonetheless affected the beginning of production, which was already on a tight schedule. If that wasn't enough of a setback, a day before the first big production meeting, the assistant director on the film decided to quit without giving any advance notice, apparently because he didn't believe that Baker would be able to succeed in shooting such a difficult film within the time frame the budget permitted. This was the day that the final draft of the shooting script arrived.

Why did the AD quit the film so near production? Most members of the Baker inner circle interpreted it as a lack of faith in the production. According to Alexis Zabé, however, the AD actually found himself in an impossible situation vis-à-vis the production. He argues that "literally, the script was not shootable in the time we had to shoot it—that's the reality."[15] The problem was that the script required fifty-seven days of shooting, whereas the budget permitted only thirty-five days. Baker was willing to deal with the situation as best he could, but Zabé claims that during the preproduction of the film, this was the "elephant in the room" that no one was addressing. The AD believed that he had been given an impossible task, which is what caused him to quit. Zabé agrees that there was no way that the film could have been completed in the allotted time. He explains that the first assistant director has to "own the schedule." Zabé comments, "I felt sorry for him, honestly, because, as the first AD, that's your responsibility that the movie is finished on time."[16]

Despite the disruption that the AD's quitting caused to the production, Zabé considers it very beneficial for the film in the long run. Baker's improvisational process of making films can be taxing on someone responsible for scheduling a production. How can you plan something that seems like a perpetual work in progress? It forces a choice: you are either a believer or not. If a professional crew member is used to working on more conventional shoots—commercials or television—Baker's open-ended approach might not inspire full confidence.

The members of the Baker team, however, have implicit trust in him as a filmmaker. He has a proven track record, after all. He has shown great instincts and an uncanny ability to take advantage of serendipitous events. Their faith, in part, has to do with the fact that they know that he edits his own films, which Baker has come to believe is 50 percent of directing. In an article on editing in *MovieMaker*, he explains, "I once insulted a lot of directors by saying that editors should be credited as co-directors. I've now changed my statement: For *my* kind of filmmaking, editing is 50 percent of directing. It's such a strong signature on the film. You're basically in charge of pacing; I literally rewrite in post-production."[17] Alex Coco claims that when Baker is shooting a scene, such as the one where Dicky moves out of the motel, he is already editing it in his head.[18]

In some sense, his process of developing screenplays out of characters and a particular place presents a model for alternative scripting. Kevin Chinoy suggests, "It's almost as if Sean is making films by prototyping."[19] By this he means that during production the entire film is in a state of continual revision. Chinoy seems to agree that "for these kinds of stories, this is the best way to work."[20] Gilles Mouëllic understands unpredictability to be a central tenet of this more open way of working. He writes, "In improvised filmmaking each decision reached in the course of the creative process seems designed to release unpredictable forces on set and to turn each shot into an event in itself and not the *representation* of an event."[21]

Alexis Zabé strongly defends Baker's open and improvisational approach to making a film. He does not see the fact that Baker had an evolving script for *The Florida Project* to be at all risky. In fact, he views it as quite the opposite. He observes:

> I find in creative processes that you have to have a certain degree of openness; you have to welcome a certain degree of chaos in the process. If you get too attached to a plan or a preconceived idea, then you miss out on a lot because it's a living process, and the story itself is talking back to you as you're telling it. I'd say it's not risky—it's riskier to be so certain.[22]

The loss of the AD nevertheless threw the production into additional chaos. A new one had to be hired immediately on short notice, which meant that whomever they hired would not be up to proper speed. The film was rescheduled to start on Monday, June 27, but it officially began on June 30, causing the production to lose three days of shooting. The delay had serious implications because they only had Willem Dafoe for a set period of time due to his having other commitments, and the child actors had to begin school by mid-August. For a production shoot that was scheduled to be only thirty-five days, this would be cutting it very close.

The production itself proved difficult for a number of reasons, including the fact that much of the film was being shot in a large motel that was fully operational. An extraordinary heat wave near the beginning of production wreaked havoc. It was necessary to take great precautions to keep the cast and crew hydrated. There was special concern for the child actors because the production was responsible for their welfare. But there were additional problems that surfaced almost immediately. Baker was used to working with very small crews and shooting his films with more of a guerilla-style approach. The bigger budget meant that for the first time Baker was working with a professional union crew, which wasn't necessarily suited to his more improvisational sensibility.

As Alex Coco, Baker's assistant, explains, "The Baker inner circle is a very tight-knit group."[23] Baker and Bergoch were college friends. Kevin Chinoy is the older brother of the director's college roommate. Shih-Ching Tsou and Baker share a long history together, going back to his very first feature, *Four Letter Words*. Stephonik Youth is Baker's sister. Samantha Quan is his current partner. Alexis Zabé, the director of photography, and Coco previously worked with him on *Snowbird*. The members of his team have a unique way of participating in the films. Baker values their input and feedback. The co-screenwriter and acting coach normally do not hold privileged positions on the sets of commercial films. Baker, however, wanted them there because he implicitly trusts their judgment, along with that of the others in his inner circle. He relies on them to grasp what is needed in a particular situation.

This inner group can be viewed as constituting Ian Macdonald's concept of a SIWG (Screen Idea Work Group). The director, co-screenwriter, producers, production designer, director of photography, and director's assistant all shared a commitment to the screen idea of *The Florida Project*, which they understood to be a fluid and evolving process. The screen idea was not always something that was written down. Some of it was, of course—there was a shooting script—but Baker did not commit all potential ideas to paper, and some were being discovered while shooting the film. The improvisatory aspects didn't much matter to the SIWG members because they understood the essential screen idea behind the project. Yet this was not necessarily the case with many members of the larger union crew, who had very different and more conventional expectations of how motion pictures are made professionally.

Most professional crews have a hierarchical structure. They operate according to a military-like chain of command. Each member has her or his very specific job to do on set. Because the Baker team is used to working together as a small, cohesive group, they tend to operate differently. According to Coco, the Baker team would often make certain decisions more collectively as a small group of confidants—a number of them had producer credits for that very reason—but the larger production team would often learn about them secondhand.[24] As a result, the union crew sometimes resented the fact that they were not in the loop or consulted when it came to important decisions that were being made, especially when those decisions resulted in changes that affected the shooting schedule.

Baker at times confounded the union crew by making last-minute changes in shooting. As Kevin Chinoy explains, "His process is that he'll show up and realize he'll want to shoot it differently to the way we had initially planned."[25] In the original script, for example, Halley deteriorated during the course of the film as a result of continued substance abuse, but Baker decided to change Halley's character arc midstream during the production, which altered the film in a major way and caused a number of scheduling problems. In addition, filming in muggy Florida during the hot summer months of July and August made the shoot even more difficult, especially because of frequent thunderstorms. The script changes and weather issues proved taxing in terms of keeping the production on schedule.

Regarding the difficulties the production experienced, Stephonik Youth, despite her confidence that they would succeed in the end, confided, "We were walking on eggshells—that's what it felt like."[26] It didn't help matters that many members of the union crew remained openly skeptical, which made working conditions that much more difficult for the Baker crew. Youth indicates, "I felt like the whole time people were telling us, 'This isn't going to work. What are you guys doing?' "27

In *Under the Rainbow*, Baker exults in the fact that a giant rainbow occurred during production and they were somehow able to film it before it disappeared, thereby saving the $25,000 it would have cost the production to resort to CGI in order to get the same shot. But it was extremely hard to get the union crew to alter the shooting schedule on such short notice, even if it was to get an incredible shot that was actually needed but was originally planned as a costly special effect.

On *Tangerine*, Baker had a bare-bones crew, so it was easy for him to mobilize them when he sought to take advantage of some serendipitous event. On *The Florida Project*, it was hard to get union crew members to change directions quickly. That is simply not the way they are used to working. For Baker, it was more like trying to pilot a cruise ship than a speed boat. For large union crews, altering a set shooting schedule on short notice invariably causes problems. It was difficult even for the Baker crew. When the rainbow appeared, Stephonik Youth was under incredible pressure. She had been creating the lived-in look on the balconies of the exterior of the Magic Castle through meticulous production design. And now this look suddenly needed to be recreated at a moment's notice.

Earlier in *Under the Rainbow*, Baker announces, nearly two weeks into the shoot, that he needs to alter and rewrite the script. He tells Chris Bergoch, "Last night I had like a big-picture moment, and I realized that based on what we shot, on the performances, on everything, I was going in the wrong direction with her [Halley] becoming a full-out junkie."28 Even though hard-core drug abuse was a major fact

of life in the motels for the homeless and something that he
wanted to highlight, Baker had suddenly come to the realization that it was not necessary for either Halley's character
or the story, even though that was what had been previously
scripted. Baker also indicates that the violent confrontation in
which Halley attacks Ashley can take place at the door to her
room rather than publicly at the swimming pool.

The entire drug arc was changed because Baker feared
that Halley's hard-core drug use would cause her to lose
the sympathy of the audience. Viewers would no doubt perceive her as an unfit mom, which would in many ways justify
Moonee being taken from her by the DCF. Yet there was also
an attendant benefit to Baker's decision, because it meant
that many scenes no longer had to be filmed. This turned out
to be advantageous to a film that was being made on such
a tight schedule. According to Alexis Zabé, "That day, ten
days of shooting were eliminated in an instant with just that
decision . . . so the scenes where Halley's buying drugs, using
drugs, feeling horrible because she used drugs—all those
scenes were eliminated from the script."[29]

This caused Baker, Bergoch, and Coco to spend the week-
end rewriting and reorganizing the script, using sticky notes
to reshuffle the scenes based on changes they were making. According to Coco, this involved a complicated process
of "changing, rewriting, adding scenes, taking away scenes,
and reordering scenes."[30] After they finished, they briefed
Shih-Ching Tsou and Samantha Quan about changes, so that
they could check for any discrepancies in the new order of the
scenes. The effect of the changes, however, was "to screw up
the numbering of the scenes."[31] This became so complicated
that scenes had to be completely renumbered, which meant

that all the logs were off, which caused the union crew to become incredibly upset. In the same BTS film, Baker also indicates that he has figured out the scenes involving Caleb Landry Jones, who plays motel manager Bobby's son, Jack, but adds, "They're in my head, not on paper yet."[32]

The script kept undergoing revisions during shooting. Alexis Zabé admits that there were so many different script versions that at some point he stopped reading them because he wasn't sure they were ever actually going to shoot the material. Yet he saw this as a completely positive development. He remarks, "That was what made the process so cool and beautiful and amazing—that the movie we shot wasn't the movie we started out shooting."[33] He insists that they were simply reacting to the story in an open way rather than thinking about the production itself or trying to eliminate days. Zabé explains, "At the end of the day, the first AD quitting was the best thing that could have happened to us at that point, because then we had the freedom to shoot the movie we needed to shoot. The only thing the production cared about was that we finish it by day thirty-five."[34]

Zabé emphasizes the importance of the improvisatory process of *The Florida Project*. He argues that what resulted, in fact, turned out to be very different from the film that would have been made if Baker had spent five days trying to rework the shooting script so that it could be shot in thirty-five days. Zabé claims not to be sure what that film might have looked like, and instead underscores the importance of the process itself. He comments, "And the story was alive as we were telling it, and—as anything that is alive will do—it will evolve and it will change."[35] The breakdown in the schedule meant that Zabé often didn't know exactly what they would be shooting until that very morning. He had already worked with Baker on *Snowbird*, so he was actually very comfortable with Baker's much looser method of working.

Baker admits that he invariably alters his ideas during shooting. It is partially a result of the improvisatory way he works. "At any moment," he told an interviewer, "I'll be inspired by something happening on the other side of the parking lot and say, 'I'm not going to stick to the schedule right now, I'm going off schedule to grab something that is much more interesting and that's like a happy accident.'"[36] Baker also openly acknowledges that it causes a great deal of stress and division on an actual production. According to the director, "It was something that almost caused this film to shut down halfway through because people thought I was rogue and crazy."[37] The situation became so tense that one crew member, for instance, filed a grievance against Baker for moving some pieces of camera equipment when it started to rain.

Other members of the crew balked at all the spontaneous changes that were being made during the course of the film. This is understandable because it violates established protocol. According to Zabé, some members of the crew were less flexible than others, but he insists that it had nothing to do with whether an individual was union or not. As he puts it, "It had more to do with personality and how someone was used to working, and how open and flexible someone was. Some people were rolling with it, and some weren't."[38]

Like Baker, Zabé is used to working with a small, hand-picked crew who all are working on the film "for the same reason." He admits, however, that the dynamic often changes on larger-budget films, especially ones that are not being shot in close proximity to home. Some crew members are not necessarily invested in the project in the same way and view working on a production simply as a job that brings a paycheck. Zabé contends that he could have brought his own crew from Los Angeles, which would have made the shoot much easier on Baker. There simply wasn't the budget, however, to import a crew from the other coast, and, as might be expected, there were additional pressures on the production to use a Florida-based crew. Baker and others give credit to Zabé and his easygoing personality for helping to smooth over some of the more contentious issues that developed with the larger crew during production.

It never bothered the DP when Baker decided to change the shot for whatever reason, and he did his best to get other crew members to understand the advantages of Baker's improvisational approach, especially in terms of the film's underlying aesthetic of documentary realism. Zabé muses, "Reality sometimes has more surprises for you. You've got to make those work to your advantage."[39] He is used to working with more unorthodox and free-spirted directors, such as Carlos Reygadas and Sebastián Silva. In discussing Baker as a director, Zabé comments, "I find that he has all the qualities to make a great director, which are: he has clarity of vision, but openness of mind and heart. So that's all you really need. Once you have that, that's amazing. What else do you want?"[40]

Zabé offers unsolicited praise for Baker, especially for his commitment to the crew with whom he's telling the story and for his real involvement in the community. The DP notes that Baker is always willing to listen to the input of all the members of the team he has assembled. Zabé insists that he works in a similar way with the camera crew he supervises. He doesn't tell them specifically what to do or how to do their jobs, but simply throws out ideas and suggestions. Zabé observes, "What's interesting is that, in Spanish, the word for script is 'guión,' which is related to 'guide.' So I think that's why it might be easier to understand that it's only a guide and not set in stone."[41] Yet some of the crew members tended to view the script as a fixed rather than fluid document.

According to Alex Coco, many of the impromptu shots that Baker insisted on taking, such as the shot of Halley smoking a cigarette during magic hour, actually wound up being included in the final film. Yet they were disparaged by certain crew members, who were more interested in keeping the production on schedule and making sure that they were getting the essential elements of the story. Coco contends that this indicates a lack of understanding of Baker's method of shooting. As he explains, they were "kind of making them second priority, but, for Sean's style of filmmaking, sometimes these shots are first priority—you know, finding those spontaneous moments are more important than shooting the scenes that are written in the script."[42]

Baker blames himself for the problems he had with the crew on set. He told *IndieWire*, "I learned a lot of lessons. I don't want to throw anyone under the bus except for myself. I probably went into this in a naive way, thinking that everyone was going to be able to easily jump onto my way of directing."[43] There was a learning curve for the crew members to adapt to the Baker team's unorthodox method of working. Baker was so busy with casting issues prior to the start of production that he spent less time lining up his crew members and often did not have time to vet any of the choices. This is not to suggest that working with a larger union crew was an entirely negative experience. The crew made many positive contributions to the film, as Baker readily admits, especially the grip and the sound people. This was especially true when it came to the use of a Steadicam.

Baker wondered how shot stabilization affects an audience's perceptions of a film. He was initially unsure whether using a Steadicam to follow the kids in *The Florida Project*—in the scene, for instance, where Moonee and Scooty give Jancey a tour of the motel rooms of the various residents at the Magic Castle—would work if he had to create jump cuts of the long takes in the editing room. Baker asked Alex Coco to perform an experiment by cutting up long-take Steadicam shots from Paul Thomas Anderson's *Hard Eight* (1996). When Baker looked at the results, he immediately knew that the Steadicam would work just fine on his film.[44]

Baker has nothing but praise for the two Steadicam operators he employed on *The Florida Project*: "We were lucky enough to work with those two guys from Miami, Osvaldo Silvera Jr. and Mike McGowan, both guys who worked on *Moonlight*. That opening *Moonlight* 360 thing, those were the guys who did our Steadicam shots. They were incredible."[45] Because Baker often had to grab shots in a documentary fashion during the shoot, he was sometimes forced to rely on Silvera and McGowan's skill and expertise. An example occurs in the scene where Bobby tries to chase away three cranes from in front of the motel. Because cranes are an endangered species, the production team had no control over the birds, so the Steadicam operator had to grab the shot while Dafoe improvised the action. As Baker observes, "And so he [Dafoe] does this thing where he's shooing them away, and our Steadicam guy just gives me that nice move up. I think we were all just in a moment where we were like, *capture this!*"[46]

Although a bigger budget brings many obvious benefits to a

production, the director sees some disadvantages to shooting with a bigger budget and much larger crew. For him, the constraints of a union production have important implications, namely that "there are rules that come with shooting on union films that make it impossible to shoot in an intimate style."[47] Baker is also critical of what he considers to be the unnecessary expense that employing a large crew involves. As an indie filmmaker at heart, he simply feels that there were a lot of positions on *The Florida Project* that weren't entirely necessary, which wasted a lot money. At times, he would have preferred not to spend the money at all, or to have spent the money on things other than crew, such as music rights or more extras.

The call sheet for the final day of production, dated August 17, 2016, can serve as an example.[48] It was essentially a day to do pickup shots involving four of the actors: Bria Vinaite and the three main child actors. A total of thirty-nine crew members were scheduled to be on set at various times during the day. This group included a transportation coordinator and two other transportation crew members. Listed are a picture car coordinator, a medic, a studio teacher (presumably for tutoring the child actors who would normally be in school), a special effects supervisor, and a special effects technician. It is understandable that, to an indie filmmaker who shot *Tangerine* with a skeletal crew on a shoestring budget with an iPhone, this would seem excessive.

Having a large crew sometimes affected the way that Baker shot certain scenes, especially when he was seeking to create a greater sense of documentary realism. He decided to approach the scenes of Halley and Moonee selling perfume to actual tourists staying at upscale hotels in a candid camera style: using telephoto lenses and microphones on the two actors and obtaining signed releases after the fact. He told *IndieWire*,

"Do you know how much more difficult that is to do when there's 40 people around you and you just want everyone to go away?"[49] Baker, for instance, struggled to fathom why the head of transportation on the production needed to be there.

Of course, when shooting on a bigger budget, more positions become needed, presumably because of the larger financial stakes involved and, hence, greater liability than a film like *Tangerine* involves. Baker still strongly believes that the film could have been made for less money and, as a result, would have been more profitable in the long run. He notes, "So what I'm trying to say is that with these small types of movies, these intimate character-study films, I don't have the need to spend that much money, but it seems that other people do."[50]

Baker has worked on commercials where the productions are what he considers "pampered."[51] The crew gets to eat the best food and stay in the best hotels. Yet that sense of privilege seems at odds with the kinds of films that he is interested in making, which are about people who are the opposite of pampered and, in fact, living very precarious and marginal lives. And he believes that somehow needs to be reflected in the production itself. For Baker, it becomes an ethical issue. He asks, "Do we need to splurge so much when we're making films about people who have nothing? It doesn't feel ethically right to me." Baker adds, "I guess I get a little disenchanted, a little disgusted by how much [money] this industry likes to waste. It's as simple as that."[52]

AND WHEN HAS YOUR SUMMER EVER BEEN PLOT-DRIVEN?

Much of *The Florida Project* focuses on the exploits of Moonee and her small group of friends, which makes it more episodic than plot-driven. As Baker explains, "For this film I wanted the audience to feel like they've spent the summer with these characters. And when has your summer ever been plot-driven? No, you're just meandering through your summer. I felt it had to be just a series of events, not bound to a plot."[53]

Moonee and Scooty sit listlessly against the bright purple motel building. Someone shouts their names. It turns out to be their friend Dicky. The camera tracks behind him as he runs toward the hotel. The film intercuts between Dicky and Moonee and Scooty, who continue to yell back to each other until he arrives to announce, "Freshies at the Future!" As Moonee and Scooty rush off with him and exit the frame, the camera remains fixed on the purple painted wall as the opening credits appear to Kool & the Gang's song "Celebration," after which the kids race past the large sign for the nearby Futureland Inn. Three large rockets create a triangular border for the sign: the two on each side are marked "USA" and "Canada," while "Entrance" is written on the third one below, which points in the direction of the motel. In large letters, the sign ironically announces, "Stay in the Future Today."

Dicky, Moonee, and Scooty race toward the Futureland Inn.

Once at the other motel, the three kids crouch down as Dicky fingers a blue vehicle to attack. The three proceed to climb the stairs and run the length of the balcony, and all begin to spit on the car below. In one frontal shot, the three kids are framed behind the spokes of the balcony railing as if they are in a jail cell, an image that seems to comment visually on their delinquency, or perhaps the possible futures that await them as adults. After the car's owner, a Latina named Grandma Stacy (Josie Olivo), steps out of the room to smoke a cigarette, she suddenly notices what the kids are doing. When she complains, the three kids defiantly resort to foul language. Dicky yells, "Go home, you rat-shit bitch." Moonee adds, "You are shit!" As Grandma Stacy's shy young granddaughter, Jancey, emerges from the room to investigate, their spit lands on her.

After being spit on from above, Jancey is comforted by Grandma Stacy.

As they race back home, Dicky is spotted by his father (Edward Pagan) from the balcony as he runs past. Dicky's dad yells, "Get your ass upstairs right now," while Moonee and Scooty head back to the Magic Castle and continue upstairs to Moonee's motel room. Since the door to her room is locked, Moonee proceeds to slide the window open, climbs through it, and opens the door from the inside to allow Scooty to enter. The camera frames a close shot of Halley smoking a blunt and watching television in the foreground, as the two kids immediately jump on the bed with their shoes on. In one of the only instances of Halley attempting to exert parental authority, she tells them to take their shoes off.

After Grandma Stacy reports what occurred to Bobby, the two of them knock at the door. Moonee answers, then quickly slams it shut. When Halley goes to investigate, Bobby tells her to work it out with Grandma Stacy and threatens to evict her for smoking in the room. The brief scene depicts the antagonistic, love-hate relationship between the two of them. She responds to him like she would to any authority figure. Bobby acts like an annoyed parent and treats Halley like a delinquent child.

The Florida Project has a slow narrative build. This stems from Baker not wanting to have a conventional dramatic structure, but also from needing to introduce so many different characters: Moonee, Scooty, and Dickey, as well as the new kid, Jancey. The children are immediately shown getting into mischief and using foul language to Grandma Stacy. We are also introduced to Halley, who is watching television and getting high, which serves to highlight her complete lack of supervision of Moonee. The misbehavior of the kids also brings the hotel manager, Bobby, into the picture. The conflict between Bobby and Halley appears to be a long-standing one, as is evident from his quick threat to evict her. The setup also establishes the film's two major settings: the Magic Castle and the nearby Futureland Motel.

Once Halley reluctantly agrees with Moonee and Scooty washing the car's windshield and hood, the two kids head to the laundry room to get a roll of paper towels from a Latina named Bertha (Rosa Medina Perez) who works there. As Halley, Moonee, Scooty, and Grandma Stacy walk over to Futureland, we learn that Grandma Stacy's two granddaughters, Jancey and her younger sister, Luci, are now under her care. She explains to Halley, "My daughter made me a grandmother when she was fifteen, so I'm looking after them until she stops acting like her stupid father." Her remarks suggest how an established pattern of behavior manages to get repeated generationally.

When Moonee and Scooty turn the washing of the car's windshield into a game, Grandma Stacy insists that the job is supposed to be "work," but Halley defends the fact that the kids are having fun, which undercuts the punitive aspect of the task. To Grandma Stacy's dismay, Moonee gets Jancey to join in the cleanup effort, thereby creating a new friendship. As Grandma Stacy argues with Halley, claiming that the kids were "very disrespectful," the two women surprisingly bond over a cigarette, so that in the end Grandma Stacy decides, "I need to lighten up, I need to light up, and I need to get laid." Halley agrees with her, remarking, "Same here, girl. I feel you." These last lines do not appear in the screenplay.

The scene of the car washing has a twofold purpose. Halley refuses to see anything wrong in the children's behavior. She instead wants to turn the act of restitution into a fun time for the kids, which shows that she misses the point entirely. Nevertheless, the cleanup effort allows Moonee and Scooty to become friends with Jancey, once she decides to assist them against her grandmother's wishes. This marks the beginning of her entry into Moonee's orbit of friends. The fact that the two adults quickly settle their dispute has an expository function, but, like all good exposition, its import will only become evident at a later point in the film.

Moonee and Scooty sit against a building containing a mural showing kids and oranges—part of the "Welcome to Florida" sign on the Orange World Gift Shop—until Scooty's mother, Ashley, signals to them. They run to the back of Waffle Home (a play on Waffle House, which declined permission to let the production shoot in the restaurant) to pick up a doggie bag of leftover food. Moonee mentions that her mom wants to know if Ashley is planning to go to the OBT (Orange Blossom Trail) that night. Ashley answers that it's Saturday, so she's up for it. The kids then bring the food back to Halley, and the three of them sit on a picnic table and give middle fingers to a helicopter full of tourists from Disney World that flies loudly overhead.

Halley, Moonee, and Scooty eat leftovers at the picnic table.

Halley's desire to have a good time is depicted when she and Ashley go to the OBT later that night. Although we see the two women having fun away from the kids, most viewers won't necessarily understand the reference to the Orange Blossom Trail. The seven-mile strip in Orlando is a notorious epicenter for drugs and prostitution, but it is also a place where ordinary people gather on weekends. The scene at the OBT shows the two women socializing, ordering food, dancing together, and discussing their dead-end job situations. Ashley complains about being passed over for the manager position at the restaurant. She suggests that if she gets to be a manager, she'll be sure to hire Halley first thing.

According to Kevin Chinoy, the genesis for that scene occurred when they were scouting locations.[54] It was late one night and they wanted to grab a bite to eat at a restaurant on the Orange Blossom Trail. The restaurant turned out to be closed, but they discovered a lively area consisting of food trucks, drag races, lots of motorcycles, and people who were partying with six-packs of beer. Baker was so taken with the social activity he fortuitously discovered that he decided to work the location into the film. Chinoy uses this as an example of Baker's approach of incorporating what he finds around him into his films. Since the production couldn't get a permit to shoot there, they put up posters notifying everyone about the movie, and Baker shot the scene using a handheld, documentary style.

After this, Halley goes to Social Services and meets with a case worker to discuss her efforts to seek employment. As Moonee plays with a doll, Halley complains that she got fired as an exotic dancer for refusing to provide extra services to clients in the back room. The dialogue very closely adheres to that contained in the screenplay. Halley delivers the lines in a speedy tempo: "Most of those rachet-ass bitches were doing extras . . . you know, in the back room. I'm not doing extras. I'm dancing for tips. That's what I do. I said no . . . two days later with no warning Hector fired me . . . after not letting me up on stage all fucking night. Fucking bullshit!" The case worker suggests that Halley needs to work thirty hours or it will affect her TANF (Temporary Assistance for Needy Families) benefits. Halley claims to have job applications up and down the Route 192 strip. She becomes upset, wonders why she even went there, and asks the case worker if she can at least give her bus passes.

The film provides little backstory for Halley. We never find out, for instance, what happened to Moonee's father. Baker is less concerned with how she managed to get herself into this predicament than with her actual plight: that of a single mom with a young kid and without the necessary skills or means of support. The early scenes, such as the one with her case worker, provide enough background information to understand her character. We learn the reason why she lost her job and can't seem to land another one, which will affect her eligibility to receive government assistance. In interviews, Baker has indicated that he tries to eliminate exposition whenever possible. Yet the scene has an important function that is not obvious: it establishes a major character arc for Halley regarding the position she takes on sex work.

Moonee and Scooty march past the rocket sign at the entrance to Futureland. They stop at Dicky's room, but his father has grounded him for a week for what they did to Grandma Stacy's car. The two are disappointed, but Moonee has a bright idea. They visit Grandma Stacy's room and ask if Jancey can come out and play with them. Grandma Stacy is initially skeptical, but Moonee assures her, "Your daughter is safe in my hands." Instead of going back to the Magic Castle, Scooty and

Moonee take Jancey on an excursion. In a wide shot, they walk past Orange World, a building in the shape of a giant orange, and the Jungle Falls Gift Shop. Jancey asks, "Don't you think we're going too far?" Moonee answers, "No, just come on. Don't be a loser!" Jancey responds, "Don't call me that" as she struggles to keep up with the other two.

The three kids walk into a wide shot of the Twistee Treat, an ice cream stand in the shape of a giant cone. Moonee announces to Jancey, "This is where we get free ice cream." They ask a man at the counter for money. As they sit counting the coins they've hustled, they realize they're short. The three kids approach a woman and her daughter who have just gotten ice cream and ask for money. Scooty tells the woman, "And the doctor said we have asthma and gotta eat ice cream right away." When the woman gives them some money, the three kids share the cone, passing it back and forth on the way back to the Magic Castle.

Moonee and Scooty proceed to give Jancey a tour of their motel. The two provide their new friend with a running commentary about the residents who inhabit the different rooms. Moonee, for instance, tells her, "The man in here gets arrested a lot." Stopping at another door, she remarks, "This woman in here thinks she's married to Jesus." During the tour, she also informs Jancey, "And no one uses the elevator because it smells like pee." The children accept this world as an ordinary fact of life.

Moonee and Scooty also introduce Jancey to mischief. Moonee shows Jancey the rooms that are off-limits before she announces excitedly, "But let's go anyway." A shot of Bobby working at his computer suddenly goes dark. He yells, "Fuck!" The film cuts to a wide shot of the exterior of the motel, as various doors begin to open and complaints from the sweltering residents about the electrical outage start to be heard. Upon investigating, Bobby discovers that someone flipped the power switch. After fixing the problem, in a low-angle shot, he strides out triumphantly to cheers from the residents. Someone shouts, "We love you, Bobby!" He yells back, "I love you too!" Bobby wants to be loved and appreciated, but his glory is only a temporary victory in an otherwise grim environment that he desperately struggles to maintain.

An older female resident wearing a cowboy hat (later introduced as Gloria) already wants a discount due to the power outage as she argues with the clerk, Amber (Patti Wiley). Bobby chooses to ignore them as he heads into his office. In reviewing the security tapes, he learns that Moonee, Scooty, and Jancey are the culprits, as he sees them enter the utility room on the monitor. The film cuts to a shot of the three children playing on the bed in Halley's room. After the kids avoid answering the loud knock at the door, Bobby yells to them from outside. Halley turns to the kids and exclaims, "Fucking A! What did you do now?"

Bobby explains what the kids did and threatens to evict Halley if it happens again. He tells her, "It's only the second week of the summer, and there's already been a dead fish in the pool." Moonee defends herself by exclaiming, "We were doing an experiment. We were trying to get it back alive." Bobby is also upset with them for throwing water balloons at tourists. He warns her, "You don't fuck with tourists!" Halley turns to Moonee and comments sarcastically, "Oh my god, this is unacceptable. I've failed as a mother. Moonee…you've disgraced me." Bobby also lectures Halley about taking responsibility for the kids in her care, but she has no parenting skills whatsoever. She is incapable of serving as any type of parental role model for Moonee—discipline is not part of her vocabulary. Bobby ends up asking Halley for the rent money. When she finally manages to come up with it, he leaves.

Many scenes in *The Florida Project* do not necessarily advance the plot of the film, but they serve other functions. The next scene of the young honeymooners who mistakenly booked a room at the Magic Castle instead of one in the Magic Kingdom serves as a good example. Baker moved the scene earlier because he felt that it provided expository information that was necessary to understand the plight of the hidden homeless. The scene shows how the presence of homeless children in the rundown motels on Highway 192 registers on Disney "guests" who are there to experience the insular world of the theme park and its manufactured happiness.

Brazilians' love of Disney World and their heavy presence at the theme park is a cultural phenomenon that has been well documented in numerous travel books. When Randy Moore secretly shot *Escape from Tomorrow* (2013) in Disney World and Disneyland, for example, he wanted to cast Brazilians in the roles of the two teenage women with whom the main character, Jim White (Roy Abramsohn), becomes obsessed. Moore had to change them to French when he was unable to find Brazilian actors to fill the roles. Chris Bergoch, who goes to Disney World quite regularly, was extremely familiar with the attraction that the theme park holds for Brazilians. In addition, it seems inevitable that some tourists, especially those from foreign countries, would book motels along Highway 192 by accident, given their proximity to the Walt Disney World resort. In many ways, this highway strip, with its tacky gift shops, has become the knock-off version of the trappings of the famous amusement park.

In the scene of the newlyweds having booked the wrong

hotel, the husband tells Bobby that Brazilians love Disney. His new Brazilian wife has been coming to Disney World since she was a kid, and her dream was to have her honeymoon at one of the Disney resort hotels. When Moonee and Scooty struggle to bring in their heavy luggage from the curb, she exclaims in Portuguese, "What are these stray children rummaging about? This is a welfare, slum hotel. We're spending our honeymoon in a gypsy project? Find another place!"

The scene depicts how Disney tourists or outsiders might view the theme park's hidden underside, especially the homeless children. The woman has visible disdain and immediately chooses to turn them into the Other. Due to their young age, Moonee and Scooty are not yet aware of how they are perceived by adults like the Brazilian bride. Her stigmatizing of them is hidden by the fact that she is speaking a foreign language that neither child can understand. Yet we know from documentaries and articles about homeless children that their situation will eventually cause them to feel shame and embarrassment as they grow older, and their chances in life will be severely stunted as a result.

From outside the front doors of the motel, Moonee and Scooty watch the upset young couple and their annoyed taxi driver as they argue inside. Scooty comments that the wife is pretty. Moonee agrees with him, but adds, "I feel bad for her. She's about to cry. I can always tell when adults are about to cry." Ironically, Moonee is the one who feels empathy for the distressed woman rather than the other way around.

The scene of the newlyweds makes a statement about the nature of Disney World itself. Art historian Cher Krause Knight contrasts Disneyland with Disney World and discusses the latter as an environment that Walt Disney deliberately planned to be insulated and cut off from the everyday world. She writes, "In California, the inconsistencies of daily life kept trespassing on his park; in Florida he made certain to block out any external distractions. In a way, Disney World is placeless: despite its national and regional associations, its buffered insulation distinctly separates it from the outside world."[55]

Walt Disney apparently learned from the mistakes he made in creating Disneyland. After considering a number of different locations, Disney settled on the Orlando, Florida, area, using dummy corporations to buy 27,443 acres of swampy land for $5.5 million dollars.[56] The secrecy was necessary to keep prices from becoming inflated if the true buyer and intentions of the project (referred to by Disney executives as "Project X" and "the Florida Project") were discovered. Why did Disney need to buy such a vast amount of land for the proposed theme park? Knight explains, "He intended to use most of the land as a buffer for his resort so that all of the chaos, visual disharmonies, and pressures of the outside world would not trespass upon his orderly microcosm."[57] Although the acreage of Disney World is "twice the size of Manhattan," history has proven that it has not provided enough of a buffer, as the motels housing homeless children along the tacky corridor of Route 192 attest.

Bobby's boss, Narek (Karren Karagulian), becomes irritated as he watches church volunteers distributing day-old bread and other bakery goods to the homeless residents of the Magic Castle. These include a woman with a black eye (a victim of domestic abuse) and Moonee, who manages to grab three items. Narek tells Bobby to ask the young church workers to move their van to the back of the motel, where it will be less noticeable. As a slumlord, Narek can exploit the homeless by taking their rent money, but he would prefer them to be invisible. The scene also shows the pressures that Bobby faces from his boss in navigating the situation with the residents.

In the next scene, we get further insight into Bobby's character. His son, Jack, helps him move a mattress from one of the motel rooms. When they remove the headboard, it becomes obvious that there is an infestation of bedbugs. Jack becomes irritated that Bobby didn't alert him to the problem beforehand; if he had known, he would have worn gloves. Jack mocks Narek, and indirectly his father, for spending so much money on painting the motel rather than on an exterminator. Bobby criticizes Jack for the way he's taping the mattress with plastic, insisting that he use longer strips of duct tape. The two men move it downstairs without saying a word and place it in the dumpster. The scene exemplifies the underlying tension between Bobby and his son, which will surface in a later scene. Afterward, we watch as Bobby lights his cigarette with an old-fashioned lighter on the balcony, just before the lights come on in the motel behind him. As the camera moves to frame him more closely, he takes a couple of deep drags.

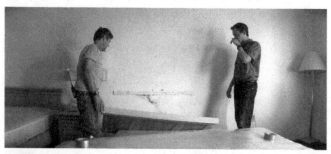

Bobby and his son, Jack, move an infested mattress from one of the motel rooms.

In the shooting script, Bobby has a brother, Kenn, but the brother transforms into a son, Jack, in the final film. Baker actually went into production without knowing exactly what those scenes would entail. In order to make that major change in characters, Baker must have had that possibility in mind prior to shooting the film. He had already noted a resemblance between Willem Dafoe and Caleb Landry Jones when he first saw Jones in Brandon Cronenberg's *Antiviral* (2012). When Baker finally decided to change the brother character into a son after production had already started, he immediately knew which actor he needed to cast. According to Baker, "And then I was like, well, if it's that—it's gonna be Caleb. You know, and I happen to know him from the Safdie Brothers. I called them and I asked them what he's like to work with (on *Heaven Knows What*) and after that it was a very simple decision at that point to cast him."[58]

The decision to turn the brother character into a son makes a great deal of sense in terms of Bobby's character. The hotel manager serves as a surrogate parental figure to Moonee and Scooty. In a sense, Bobby is looking after them when they play in and around the hotel, which he perceives to be part of his job. Ashley works at the waffle restaurant, so she's not able to watch Scooty. Halley is perhaps supposed to be keeping an eye on him, but it is Bobby who repeatedly attempts to remind Halley about her parental responsibilities to the kids. Yet, as we learn from his interactions with Jack, Bobby has his own struggles as a parent.

Moonee and Scooty enjoy annoying Bobby. They show up when he and Jack are removing the mattress, but he tells them to beat it. They share an ice cream cone in the motel lobby as he eyes them with folded arms while shaking his head, before it eventually melts and spills on the floor. When it does, he immediately chases them out. As Scooty and Moonee sit outside, they hear the sound of a door slam, which draws their attention to something offscreen. Scooty yells, "Gloria!" The two of them jump up and get Dicky, and the three of them run to get Jancey from her room. We watch as the four kids climb up the stairs of the motel to the third floor. One of the more colorful characters living at the Magic Castle turns out to be an eccentric older woman in a patriotic western hat named Gloria (Sandy Kane, a.k.a. the "Naked Cowgirl"). She appeared earlier in the film wanting a discount after the power outage, but her back was turned toward us. Her voice, however, is unmistakable.

Gloria insists on sunbathing topless by the swimming pool, much to the delight of the motel kids. In one of the film's tour-de-force shots, the camera tracks along as the four kids run across the length of the extremely long balcony of the motel in order to catch a glimpse of her bare breasts. The camera movement across the spoked railing, in combination with the myriad lines of the roof tiles, creates a magical stroboscopic effect. As the kids watch Gloria, they laugh hysterically and chant "boobies" multiple times. They also comment on the size of her large breasts before Bobby arrives to chastise Gloria for exposing herself to the children, who continue to watch her from the balcony. Jancey asks, "Does this happen all the time?" Moonee answers excitedly, "Yep, and it's great!" Baker cuts back and forth between the kids and Bobby and Gloria at the pool. Moonee, in a humorous wordplay, yells, "Bobby booby!" He shouts up to the kids, "Go back to your rooms!"

Bobby confronts Gloria for sunbathing topless in front of Moonee and her pals.

Bobby ends up covering up Gloria's breasts as she indignantly but playfully complains that he has molested her. Scooty yells, "Hey, Gloria. Rub your boobs on his face." Offscreen, Bobby shouts for them to get the hell out of there. The scene with Gloria once again fails to advance the plot but instead provides a humorous glimpse of the kinds of people who reside in the budget motels. For Bobby, who sees his job as protecting the children, this incident is another routine annoyance, but for the kids, it provides an entertaining spectacle as well as a sense of mischief and adventure.

What might not be obvious is that Baker manipulated this scene in postproduction. There is a shot in which we watch the heads of the four kids—Moonee, Jancey, Scooty, and Dicky—in different quadrants, as they watch Gloria from the balcony of the third floor of the motel. The timing of the kids' heads moving up and down in the frame, which Baker wanted for "comic timing," proved difficult to synchronize while shooting the scene. His solution was to achieve the effect in postproduction through CGI, creating what Baker describes as the equivalent of "whack-a-mole."[59] In terms of other CGI effects, Baker also removed an annoying smudge on the purple building at the beginning of the film. According to Baker, they also "swapped out skies in a couple of places," when the preferred take did not match the color of the sky in the rest of the scene.[60]

Afterward, Moonee and Scooty amuse themselves by making sounds into the whir of a circular electric fan. Another motel worker, Patrice (Terry Allen Jones), walks in and tells them, "Kids, out!" on his way to the back office. Amber complains to Bobby about the broken ice machine, but Bobby announces that it can't be fixed. As he starts to head out, he turns and says, "Patrice, keep your eyes on 151. There's been traffic in and out of there all day." When Patrice reacts with exasperation, Bobby indicates that he'll take care of it in the morning. As Bobby heads out the door, he turns his fingers into a makeshift gun and playfully shoots at Moonee and Scooty, who continue to play in the lobby. Bobby walks down to room 101 and disappears inside.

The next morning, Bobby knocks on the door of Room 151 and proceeds to evict a couple from the motel for "breaking the rules." The woman, who has blonde hair, aggressively protests that she paid for a week. Bobby threatens to call the sheriff and suggests, as a guy ushers her toward the car, "Your man knows what the story is." Although the reason is not stated directly, the short scene was set up the night before when Bobby told Patrice that there had been a lot of traffic going in and out of the room, suggesting that the couple had been dealing drugs.

Accompanied by Moonee, Halley buys wholesale perfume, which she hawks to multiple tourists staying at the more upscale motels. Moonee tells a guy pulling his luggage, "This will make all the girls flirt on you." When Halley gets back to the Magic Castle, she uses the money that she's made to pay the rent. Bobby lets her know that it's a day late. When he starts to count the money, Halley asks whether he thinks she can't count and the two of them exchange playful banter. In scenes with Bobby, Halley often plays the role of a delinquent who makes his job more difficult, even if it's clear that he feels sympathetic to her dilemma.

Shortly after this, in a low-angle shot, Dicky's father asks him if he wants to say goodbye to his room. Dicky gives high-fives to his friends in the parking lot of the Futureland Motel. It turns out that he and his single dad are moving to New Orleans. As the other kids crowd around, Dicky's father says there isn't enough room in the car for Dicky's toys, so he convinces Dicky to give them all away, promising to buy him new ones once they get to their new location. Both people and possessions are disposable to the homeless families who live in the motels.

Dicky is forced to give away his toys when he and his dad move out of the motel.

This scene is shot in a documentary style, with many more children than we see in any other scene in the film. Baker would decide the list of shots he wanted beforehand in consultation with Alexis Zabé and the AD—always those two people—and maybe some other key members of the crew, which Alex Coco would write down. They had a term for what they did in the scenes that were shot in a more documentary style: "hose it down."[61] This was shorthand for "catch as catch can," getting the key coverage they needed as quickly as possible, especially in a chaotic situation.

Alexis Zabé considers the scene of Dicky's moving out of the motel to be one of his favorites in the film because it sums up the situation of transience so succinctly on a "sensorial and emotional level."[62] He also likes it for its sense of realism. Such scenes, he believes, are a necessary complement to the more structured ones in the film. As Zabé observes, "Having these very loose and documentary-style scenes cut in with these very structured scenes makes them kind of inhabit the world, which is real."[63] In other words, scenes like Dickey moving or the earlier one in which Moonee, Scooty, and Jancey wash Grandma Stacy's car help to ground the film in documentary realism, providing a counterweight to the kids' vision of reality, which Zabé sees as being very different.

Many of the children who appear as extras in the scene of Dicky moving were actually recruited from the Paradise Motel, where Christopher Rivera lived. It comes as something of a surprise to the viewer that one of the major characters is about to disappear from the film. After all, the film began with Dicky recruiting Scooty and Moonee to spit on a new resident's car, which becomes how the trio meets Jancey. Dicky, however, gets grounded for a week for his bad behavior. This allows Jancey to become better friends with Moonee and Scooty as they introduce her to the fun aspects of life in the motels: begging money for ice cream and annoying Bobby and the residents by turning off the power. Dicky is still part of the gang as they stare at Gloria from the balcony, but circumstances suddenly force him to move away.

Rather than being portrayed in a sentimentalized manner, the departure of Dicky is presented as a matter-of-fact occurrence. Other than the kids exchanging high-fives, there are no real reaction shots of any of them expressing sadness over his departure. Moonee, who holds a bunch of toys in her arms, does not explicitly say goodbye, but rather does so indirectly by telling Dicky, "My mom said, 'Have fun.'" In fact, the kids are much more interested in getting Dicky's stash of cheap toys. Moonee, in particular, makes sure she grabs more than her fair share of them.

The decision to introduce a major character and then eliminate him was a deliberate strategy on the part of the screenwriters. They used it to show that transience is such an integral part of life for these kids. There is no stability in their lives or anything to anchor them to any specific place. Even their rooms in the motel are not permanent places of residence. After all, a motel is by definition a temporary rather than a stable dwelling. In order to stay there, as the film later shows, these homeless families, such as Halley and Moonee, must move out of their room every thirty days in order to prevent them from establishing permanent residency. If they were to establish residency, they would then qualify for tenant rights, which the motels won't allow. This was something that the screenwriters witnessed firsthand in researching the film.

A FORESHADOWING OF TROUBLE TO COME

The departure of Dicky might serve as a dramatic event, but it doesn't—in fact, nothing dramatic has really happened so far in the film. In screenwriting terms, there has not been an inciting incident or catalyst to set the story in motion, or a turning point that might send it in a very different direction. Right afterward, however, Scooty shares a secret with Moonee. He shows her a cigarette lighter with a picture of a naked lady on it. Moonee puts her hands to her mouth in surprise and laughs at the image of the naked woman. She asks Scooty whether he stole it, but he gives her a vague answer before Halley yells at them from upstairs to go and get some waffles. Astute viewers, however, could expect that the introduction of Scooty's cigarette lighter may serve a narrative function by foreshadowing trouble to come.

Scooty shows Moonee his cigarette lighter with an image of a naked lady.

After Moonee and Scooty get leftovers from Ashley at Waffle Home, the two kids eat the food with Halley at a picnic table. In the foreground of the shot, Scooty begins to "twerk." As Halley watches, she asks, "What, are you twerking over there? Let me see." As Halley makes sounds while Scooty dances, Moonee then begins to twerk in the background, shaking her rear end for the camera. Halley looks up from her cell phone and comments, "Oh, wow! You got some twerk skills, girl!" Moonee then "shakes her booty" for her mother. Moonee and Halley also perform dance moves together at other times in the film as a form of communicating with each other.

Later that evening, Halley checks to see that Moonee is asleep before she joins Ashley in the swimming pool, where Halley smokes a blunt and the women drink beer. Ashley asks Halley about a guy she's met at OBT, but Halley indicates that he is not interested in kids. That seems to be a deal-breaker for the two women. Halley complains about Moonee farting from Ashley providing too much maple syrup. As they head back to their respective rooms, Ashley yells to Halley, "Goodnight, bitch, I love you." Halley reciprocates, which establishes the warm friendship and sense of camaraderie that exists between the two women.

Moonee, Scooty, and Jancey share an ice cream cone as they sit outside the Twistee Treat. When they get yelled at by a woman from inside the ice cream stand for loitering, Scooty defiantly insists they are "paying customers." Moonee and Jancey run back into the offices at the hotel afterward and hide under Bobby's desk as he tries to work. When Scooty enters the lobby and starts to ask Amber where they are, she points to Bobby's office. When Scooty comes looking for them, Bobby motions with his head to where the two girls are hiding. After Scooty locates them, the three kids run out of the office to play.

In writing the screenplay, Baker and Bergoch were drawing on their own childhood experiences as well as specific research for the film. Many of the scenes in the film were inspired by social phenomena they observed firsthand while conducting research, such as prostitution, drug use, domestic abuse, and bedbugs. As they were scouting locations, one motel manager,

John Manning, confronted the two of them with a baseball bat. What were the two middle-aged men doing snooping around? It was obvious that he was protecting the children who lived in the motel. As soon as they left, the two screenwriters knew that they needed to have a scene like this in the movie. The suspicions of the real-life motel manager were translated into the next scene, of an elderly pedophile who wanders into the area where the kids are playing.

Bobby, who is busy painting the motel on a ladder nearby, spies a man talking to the children, immediately senses danger, and intervenes. When the man claims to be looking for a soda machine, Bobby escorts him over to one, where he forces the man to buy a can of soda. Bobby makes him take a drink and then swiftly knocks the can out of his hand. He wrestles the man and snatches his wallet from his pocket. Bobby takes out his license, identifies him as Charlie Coachman (played by local Florida actor Carl Bradfield) of Cherry Hill, New Jersey, and threatens to turn him in to the sheriff before hurling his wallet and running him off the property.

Bobby grabs the driver's license of the unwanted intruder, Charlie Coachman.

The scene functions to show Bobby's protective nature toward the children in his custody, as well as potential dangers to the young kids living in the motels. As the sound of a helicopter that swirls overhead increases in volume, this point is reinforced by a reaction shot of Moonee and Jancey, who have been observing the disturbing incident from the sidelines. According to Baker, "The pedophile scene was definitely rooted in reality. Something that kept coming up when speaking to residents and reading articles was that pedophilia is rampant because children are there. There are sex offenders living in the motels that children are living in. It was something we had to address."[64]

Baker's co-screenwriter, however, views the scene somewhat differently. In the screenplay for the film, the pedophile character is identified simply as "suspicious man." He is listed as "Charlie Coachman" in the film credits. The name is a Disney reference that Bergoch deliberately included in the script. According to Bergoch, the character is named for the Coachman in *Pinocchio* who takes the little children in order to turn them into jackasses. Despite giving the character a name that implies that he's intended to be a villain, Bergoch considers the issue of him being a pedophile to be ambiguous—an open question.

Bergoch claims to like the mystery of the character and didn't want to label him a pedophile, whereas Baker insists that pedophiles are part of the daily reality for children living in the motels. It was a case of going against the stereotype in casting Bradfield. If the scene has a slightly ambiguous note, it largely has to do with the actor's performance. There is definitely something "off" about this character, but he never actually does anything overt to the children. In both the script and film, however, his intentions are possibly conveyed by the fact that he initially approaches the children and tries to engage them by saying, "Hi, kids. You having fun?" As Bobby comes over to the picnic table where the young children are playing, the man asks a Black girl, "What's your name?"

The shooting of the scene actually caused friction between Willem Dafoe and the producer Kevin Chinoy over safety issues. The scene begins with Bobby standing high on a ladder and painting the trim of the motel. When Bobby sees the intruder, he gets distracted and knocks an entire can of white paint to the ground. It crashes and splatters below, just missing one of the residents who happens to be passing by. The guy curses at Bobby. When filming the scene, Dafoe had climbed the ladder and was ready to do the shot. According to Chinoy, the actor was thirty feet off the ground, yet the ladder had not been properly secured to the building and Dafoe was not wearing a safety harness (which would be painted out in postproduction).[65] When Chinoy insisted that this presented a safety issue, Dafoe, who was already focused on what he needed to do as an actor in the scene, balked at taking such precautions. He became very upset with the producer and an argument ensued, causing tension on the set. Given Dafoe's status as a major actor, it was hard to challenge him in the situation. Chinoy, however, believed it was his duty as a producer to do so, even if it meant temporarily alienating the production's star actor. Baker actually agrees with Chinoy that Dafoe being on an unsecured ladder so high up did pose a safety threat.

After brief scenes of Halley and Moonee selling perfume to tourists and Halley giving Moonee a bath, we see Moonee, Scooty, and Jancey in a wide shot as they walk along the highway and then past a boarded-up medical clinic. The shot lasts

A distracted Bobby accidentally spills a can of white paint on a resident below.

for nearly forty seconds. They climb through a wooden fence and do a kind of exaggerated skipping movement past one of the pink buildings of a nearby abandoned condominium complex. In an echo from earlier versions of the script, Moonee asks, "Scooty, will you marry me?" Scooty answers, "Not right now." Moonee says, "You may kiss the bride." Scooty retorts, "I said not right now." Jancey comments, "Ew. Ew." As they walk, the kids engage in funny banter back and forth. When Scooty suggests that there are alligators in the nearby grass, Moonee responds, "If I had a pet alligator, I would name mine 'Ann.'"

At the count of three, Scooty throws a rock and breaks the window of a lime-green building. This scene, which takes place inside an abandoned building, is meant to suggest that for these kids this is the equivalent of a haunted house, or nearby Disney World's Haunted Mansion. Once inside, Scooty imagines the house being hundreds of years old, and Moonee delights in pointing at white insulation on the floor and exclaiming to Jancey that it's "ghost poop." Scooty breaks a large mirror with a metal pipe and pushes a porcelain toilet bowl out the window and old furniture down the stairs. At Moonee's instigation, Scooty uses his cigarette lighter to ignite a pillow they have stuffed into the fireplace.

At Moonee's instigation, Scooty uses his lighter to set a pillow on fire in one of the abandoned condos.

Shot from a low angle behind them, the children quickly flee down the sidewalk. Realizing that they may now be in serious trouble, Moonee instructs the other two to keep it a secret. When Moonee gets upstairs at the motel, Halley tells her the old condos are on fire, but Moonee shows little enthusiasm. From a shot taken from a position behind Bobby, black smoke billows in the distance. When Scooty doesn't want to watch the fire, Ashley becomes suspicious. Grabbing his face in her hands, she confronts him and warns, "Do you want the DCF down here?" As she demands that he tell her the truth, the camera holds close on Scooty's face. His answer is left as a dangling cause—dialogue or action toward the end of a scene that creates an open question that will be answered at a later time. The function of the narrative device is to create and maintain audience interest in the story.

The fire turns out to provide entertainment for the neighborhood folks, who gather to watch the spectacle of an entire building engulfed in flames. "Aren't you excited? This is better than TV," Halley remarks to Moonee as she takes a picture of her in front of the burning structure. Halley tells her to "smile" as she takes her picture, but Moonee's mood is anything but happy. One of the spectators complains that the house was used for prostitution and shouts, "Let it burn!" Back at the Magic Castle, Bobby passes by Gloria, who is smoking a cigarette downstairs. He grubs one from her. Gloria suggests to him that the fire could be arson, adding that the abandoned condos were "so ugly, even [she] thought of burning them down."

Halley takes a photo of Moonee in front of the burning condo.

The children's inadvertent act of arson soon leads to the central dramatic conflict of the film. As a result of the incident, when Moonee shows up at Waffle Home with Jancey, Ashley stops supplying her with food and refuses to allow Scooty to play with her any longer.

In reality, the motels are far more dangerous environments than they are depicted to be in Baker's film, but we get a sense of the violence in the next scene, when a brawl erupts in the parking lot of the Magic Castle at night, providing entertainment for the residents. Halley and Moonee watch it from their balcony. Halley cheers on the fighters and takes pictures of the scuffle with her cell phone. We hear the sound of tires screeching as a car suddenly knocks one of the men onto the back of the vehicle before leaving him sprawled on the ground. While Halley continues to enjoy the spectacle below, Ashley appears disgusted and takes Scooty inside, indicating the divergent reactions of the two women. As red police lights illuminate the background, Bobby tells Patrice, "How about this? No more letting people run over other people in the fucking parking lot!"

As Halley smokes a cigarette, she tells Moonee, "Go run and get some waffles, baby. And where the fuck is Scooty?" The dangling cause is addressed when Halley visits another motel room where Scooty is staying with a neighbor while his mother is at work. Halley suggests that Moonee is going to the pool and asks whether Scooty wants to come along. The neighbor indicates that Ashley doesn't think it's a good idea. Halley responds, "The fuck does that mean?" This is left as another dangling cause, but the answer becomes apparent when Halley takes Moonee to the restaurant and confronts Ashley. The dialogue in the final film, which appears below, closely resembles what appears in the screenplay:

ASHLEY: Yeah.
HALLEY: Yeah?
ASHLEY: What do you want, Halley?
HALLEY: What's going on?
ASHLEY: What do you mean?

HALLEY: You've been telling my daughter she ain't welcome here no more.

ASHLEY: Look, she can come in here, but I can't keep
giving out free food.

HALLEY: Oh shit, am I in trouble?

ASHLEY: And I don't want Scooty hanging out with her
(looks at Moonee) or that new kid from Futureland.

HALLEY: Okay, so you ain't get in trouble. So what's goin'
on then?

ASHLEY: Nothing. Nothing to discuss.

HALLEY: Really?

ASHLEY: Really.

When Ashley refuses to discuss the matter any further,
Halley retaliates by having Moonee order anything she wants
from the menu. In an effort to further annoy Ashley, she en-
gages Moonee in a burping contest and then insists that Ashley box up all the remaining food. Before they leave, Moonee
tells Ashley, "Say hi to Scooty for me." Ashley merely glares
back at her. As Halley and Moonee walk in front of the Jungle
Falls Gift Shop, Halley slams the plastic bag of leftovers on
the ground and kicks the bag, spreading the food all over the
parking lot. Moonee asks, "Mom, why did you do that?"

In the original screenplay, Halley was supposed to hurl the
bag containing leftovers into oncoming traffic, causing a car
to screech to a halt. This became an example of an instance in
which having a large crew interfered with Baker's approach to
"guerilla" or "run-and-gun" shooting. Baker had someone all
set to drive the car in the scene. When the assistant director
became aware of what Baker was planning, he insisted that
Baker had to use a stunt driver instead and threatened to shut

Ashley informs Halley at the restaurant that she does not want Scooty to play with Moonee any longer.

Halley angrily kicks the bag of leftover food after leaving Waffle Home.

the production down if he didn't. As a result, Baker was forced to restage the scene without the food being hurled onto the highway.

It is perhaps a minor issue, but it nevertheless epitomizes the dilemma that Baker faced in shooting with a large crew. In his role as producer with attendant dual allegiance, Kevin Chinoy claims that the issue was less about the size of the crew than about safety—one similar to the issue of Dafoe on the ladder in the scene with the pedophile. Because the scene would take place on Highway 192, which is a busy thoroughfare, he insists that proper preparations would have needed to be made beforehand, including restricting traffic flow and having a stunt driver available.

As a producer who has a responsibility to the financial backers, Chinoy defends being overly concerned with issues of safety. He cites the unfortunate death of Sarah Jones, a twenty-seven-year-old second assistant cameraperson, during the filming of *Midnight Rider: The Gregg Allman Story* in 2014 as an example of a production that courted danger. On the very first day of shooting, while filming without legal permission on a train trestle over the Altamaha River in Georgia, Jones was killed when an unscheduled train operated by CSX plowed into a hospital bed that had been placed on the tracks. Jones was struck by the train, and debris from the bed injured a number of other members on the production team. The court case filed by Jones's family resulted in $11.2 million in civil damages. The film's director, Randall Miller, was convicted of involuntary manslaughter and ended up spending a year in prison, making him the "first filmmaker in history to be convicted and thrown in jail for an on-set death."[66]

Baker, of course, is well aware of the risks involved in shooting films. Yet he sees a big difference between making smaller, low-budget films and larger, more commercial ones. In recalling the shooting of *Tangerine*, for instance, he learned after the film wrapped that the actor who played the second Armenian taxicab driver (Karo) didn't have a driver's license and, in fact, had never driven before. Yet he was driving up and down Hollywood Boulevard in the film—and rather erratically at that—which could have been disastrous. On a larger, commercial shoot, the production would have checked his license beforehand. Baker reflects, "So I think that *Tangerine* was the last time I could actually get away with this way more guerrilla type of filmmaking."[67]

Meanwhile, back at the Magic Castle, Bobby is moving an ice machine with Jack. As they struggle to get the heavy metal machine into the elevator, we're immediately plunged into a family drama as Jack tells Bobby, "By the way, I told her 'Happy Birthday' from you." Bobby quickly insists, "But I didn't." Bobby wants Jack to get her on the phone and tell her he didn't. The issue of his ex-wife, Jack's mother, is obviously a highly sensitive one. It leads to an argument between the father and son. In anger, Jack returns the money that Bobby paid him and tries to quit, but Bobby talks him into at least completing the job. As the two ride the elevator together, the tension between them feels palpable.

The scene is an example of how Baker and Bergoch worked together on the screenplay. After researching during the day in Florida, the two would write together at night, with each of them writing different scenes. Bergoch originally wrote the above scene showing the conflict between Bobby and his son. Baker, however, wanted to emphasize that, despite Bobby's attempt to exert control at the Magic Castle, in his personal life he acts more like a kid than his own son. According to Bergoch, this is an example of how "a scene would often become a blend of [their] different inputs."[68]

In his screenwriting talk at BAFTA, Baker mentioned a documentary film, Jake Clennell's *The Great Happiness Space: Tale of an Osaka Love Thief* (2006), as an important influence. He cited the "character reveal" that happens halfway through the film, in which the female patrons of the male escorts at a high-end Japanese club turn out to be prostitutes. What he termed a "character reveal" is a sudden twist in how we understand a particular character. Baker indicated that it is a screenwriting technique he has used in his last three films. In *Starlet*, the character reveal occurs when the viewer suddenly figures out that Jane is actually a sex worker. The character reveal in *Tangerine* happens when the cab driver Razmik picks up a prostitute and discovers she's actually a cisgender woman. His disgust catches the viewer off guard and makes us see both his sexual proclivity—transgender sex workers—and his character in an entirely new light.

In his BAFTA talk, Baker used the scene of Bobby and Jack as an example of a character reveal in *The Florida Project*. He said, "Bobby is in a place where he so isolated, so lonely that he is paying his own son for his company," which is what is revealed in a very subtle way in this scene.[69] It shows Bobby in a very different light from the way we have perceived him up until this point. Baker claimed that this character reveal doesn't really "change the course of the plot" in any significant way but rather causes the viewer to reevaluate the character in question.[70] Baker hopes the scene forces the viewer to think about the connections between Bobby's role as a surrogate parental figure to the children in the motel and his own personal life as an estranged husband and father.

The film cuts to another scene of Halley and Moonee hawking perfume at the more upscale hotels. This time a security officer riding in a golf cart intercepts them for soliciting on private property. The scene comes across as extremely comical, even though the camera remains distant—as if it's being shot clandestinely like the other shots of the tourists at the hotel. It exploits the fact that the security guard is not actually a police

officer and that her claim to authority and power is undercut
by the fact that she's riding in a golf cart. Halley's lack of respect is obvious from their interaction. Halley tells the security
guard who is trying to detain her, "Get off your power trip.
You're riding a golf cart, okay!" A tug of war over the perfume
ends with it strewn across the pavement. As Halley quickly
leaves, she is left to explain to Moonee why she let the security guard confiscate their perfume. A frustrated Halley tells
Moonee, "It's complicated, baby. I can't get arrested again."
After Moonee complains that her mother is walking too fast,
Halley stops, puts things she's carrying into her bag, and gives
Moonee a piggyback ride.

Back at the hotel room, Moonee and Halley watch television and eat pizza together. After Moonee gets tired of watching, she asks for the iPad, but Halley announces that she sold
it. When Moonee questions why, Halley tells her, "This room
costs money." Moonee remarks to her that she likes pepperoni
on pizza—an indirect criticism of the plain pizza she's eating.
Halley responds, "Pepperoni costs money." The significance of
the loss of the stash of perfume at the hotel is made obvious in
this scene, and the fact that the two of them argue for the first
time sounds an ominous note.

GIVE US A BREAK, LADY!

It's the end of the month, and Halley and Moonee have to
move out of the Magic Castle for twenty-four hours, causing
tension between Halley and Bobby as they collect their belong-
ings and deposit them in another room. Bobby gives Halley
notice that she has until Friday to pay the rent. At the Arabian
Nights Motel, where they go to stay for a single night, Moonee

dances to what's on the television screen. It turns out that the new owners have raised the price of the room from thirty-five to forty-five dollars, causing Halley to create a commotion. She calls Bobby on the phone, referring to the new owner, a South Asian woman, and the manager, Jimmy, as "these fuckos at the Arabian!" She is outraged that the new owner has raised the price of the room. Despite her total lack of power in the situation, Halley resorts to her usual tactic, which is engaging in a full-on verbal attack. Bobby tries to placate the owner on the phone without success. Moonee stops watching TV long enough to shout, "Give us a break, lady!"

The scene cuts to a wide shot of Bobby with the colorful mural-covered Disney Gifts Outlet looming behind him. He runs along the highway median and then crosses and jogs toward us as several cars pass behind him. This shot is one that caused a great deal of controversy during production. In the screenplay, the description is succinct: "Bobby crosses Route 192 headed to the Arabian Nights." Baker very much wanted the Disney Gifts shop in the background of the shot, and it was logical for Bobby to have to cross the highway in terms of the geography of where the Magic Castle was located in relation to the Arabian Nights Motel. His jogging rather than walking across the road suggests his sense of urgency.

Baker wanted this economical shot as a necessary transition, but when the director showed up to shoot it, he was informed by the production manager that they didn't have a permit for either Route 192 or the sidewalk. It was clearly the result of some type of miscommunication, because the shot he had envisioned necessitated Dafoe crossing the highway. Dafoe, whose roots are in avant-garde theater as a member of the Wooster Group, was game to run across the highway. The location manager, however, objected on grounds that they did not have the proper permits. In addition, it was considered a huge liability to have the lead actor run across a highway without the production having control over the traffic flow and the vehicles that would drive by.

This situation epitomizes the kinds of production problems that Baker found enormously frustrating—as well as a waste of valuable time, which was at a premium. Since Baker and Zabé already had the camera set up to do the shot, Dafoe, who knew what Baker wanted, sprinted across the highway in the direction away from the camera. He stopped on the grassy median divide between the two lanes of traffic, turned around, and then jogged back, which allowed Baker to get the shot he wanted. Dafoe did this two times before the location manager became so upset that she left.

As a result of her leaving, Baker then took advantage of the situation to grab the additional sidewalk shot of Halley and Moonee walking away as the sun started to set behind the buildings in the background, causing the image to flare in the lens of the camera. According to Baker, "That was again my guerilla attitude saying, 'He [Dafoe] is a grown adult. He can cross a street. It's not illegal for him to cross the street, but it's because you guys didn't permit and because of our own insurance purposes that we cannot cross the street.'"[71] Baker insists that his actors crossed Broadway constantly during the shooting of *Prince of Broadway*, and no one ever gave it a second thought.

Yet on a larger-budget film, producers, such as Kevin Chinoy, are continually concerned with issues of safety and liability because of the great deal at risk should something happen to go wrong. As Baker observes, "It's just a different way of making a film."[72] Baker also shoots commercials, where he is comfortable letting "the machine take over." Yet his approach is very different with his own films. As he puts it, "When it comes down to my own personal projects, and something I'm personally passionate about, I want to be there. I want to be controlling it. I want to be able to shoot something on a whim. I want to be able to take advantage of spontaneity."[73] Baker contends that he wouldn't have been able to get that great shot of Halley and Moonee on the sidewalk at magic hour—not because it was dangerous, but because of the issue of not having the proper permits. Baker bristles at the thought of missing such a critical shot and admits, "That's where I sort of become that immature filmmaker who is guerrilla or nothing."[74]

In the film, Bobby arrives at the Arabian Nights in an attempt to mediate the situation, but Halley is already in the process of escalating the conflict. When he tries to pay for the difference in price for a room and the South Asian owner refuses, Halley pulls the money from her pocket and slams it on the counter. The owner refuses it and chides her: "Listen to you and your child. No wonder you are in this situation. Please leave the property. Right now, leave!" In response, Halley proceeds to spill the contents of her soda on the floor. When the woman calls her "crazy," Halley grabs Moonee by the hand, curses at the woman, and storms off in the direction of the Futureland Motel.

A series of vignettes follow. Halley spends the night in Grandma Stacy's room at Futureland, much to the delight of Moonee, who gets to stay over with Jancey. The next morning, Halley and Moonee get their possessions from the storage room and move back to Room 323. There is an extended shot of Halley from behind as she smokes a cigarette. Halley and

Moonee take swimsuit selfies, and Halley gets Moonee to take a sexy picture of her in the bathroom. Moonee and Jancey see a giant rainbow after a rainstorm. Moonee takes a bath. Halley pays the weekly rent to Bobby at the hotel desk. Bored and obviously missing his friends, Scooty stares longingly out his window. As they walk the grounds, Narek insists that Bobby notify the residents that the bikes on the balcony are violations of motel policy and need to be moved. Moonee takes another bath.

Halley, Moonee, and Jancey dance in the room. The three of them hitch a ride and celebrate Jancey's birthday with a single candle on a cupcake as a colorful fireworks display explodes in the night sky over Disney World. Moonee washes a plastic horse while taking a bath. Bobby smokes a cigarette on the balcony of the motel at night and observes a man leaving one of the rooms. Moonee and Jancey get free bread from the group of church volunteers. Moonee and Jancey eat the bread with jam in an open field, where Moonee delivers a scripted line about an uprooted tree: "Do you know why this is my favorite tree? Because it's tipped over and it's still growing." The uprooted tree with gnarled roots is an allusion to the "Tree of Life" in Disney World's Animal Kingdom, thus providing another example of how Moonee and friends create their own imaginative alternate world to that of the nearby theme park.

Ashley and Scooty go to the swimming pool. After Scooty jumps in the water, Bobby comes over and asks Ashley whether she's been fronting Halley the rent. Ashley answers, "What? Why would I do that? I don't even talk to that bitch." Meanwhile, Halley smokes a cigarette and watches from the balcony. Moonee asks if she can go swimming with Scooty, but Halley forbids it. Afterward, as Halley tickles Moonee on the bed, the phone rings. Halley tells Moonee to get ready to take a bath. Halley moves to the balcony and says, "Room 323. What kind of car are you driving?" As Moonee plays with a doll in the bathtub, we hear the sound of a door opening. A man's voice offscreen says, "Oh, there's a kid in here." Halley responds, "I told you the bathroom is off-limits!" The man answers, "I had to piss." As Halley orders the man out, Moonee, whose expression freezes, quickly closes the shower curtain.

Moonee reacts to a man coming into the bathroom while she's taking a bath.

In retrospect, the sequence of vignettes has been highly expository—even if the viewer has been unable to comprehend their import fully until now. It makes sense that Halley would have financial problems after no longer having her supply of perfume to resell. In addition, she has lost her source of left-over food from Ashley at Waffle Home. The question naturally arises: Where did she get money to pay the weekly rent to Bobby?

Yet there have been a number of clues in the above sequence of scenes. For one thing, why are there so many shots of Moonee taking a bath alone? After the first one, Halley suddenly finds the money to pay the rent to Bobby, suggesting a possible causal connection. Also, before the bath, Halley cleverly gets Moonee to engage in shooting swimsuit selfies and, in the process, she gets Moonee to take a sexy pose of her wearing a bikini in the bathroom. Although the swimsuit selfies appear to be a fun game that Halley has concocted to amuse Moonee, it shows that there is something very calculated about Halley's choice of a game, which is to get Moonee to take a sexy picture of her without arousing her young daughter's suspicions. Right before Moonee takes her picture, Halley removes the photos of Moonee that appear around the bathroom mirror. It is hard to understand the purpose of her actions at the time the shot appears. It is only later that her motivation for taking away the photos becomes apparent.

Halley gets Moonee to take a sexy picture of her in a swimsuit.

Just as Baker does not want the structure of his film to be apparent to the viewer because he believes it distracts from the emotional impact of the story, the same could be said about exposition. All films need to have a certain amount of exposition. It is a truism of screenwriting that the audience should not be aware that something occurring onscreen is overtly expository. This is also the case with Halley's motivation, not only in the swimsuit-selfie scene but in the one that precedes it. The fact that Halley's actions are calculated is suggested by the previous shot, taken from behind Halley, of her smoking a cigarette with a palm tree in the background. The shot lasts for fifteen seconds. It is the only reflective shot of her in the entire film. The sheer duration of the shot suggests that it has narrative importance. It can only subsequently be read as Halley contemplating the prospect of becoming a sex worker in order to pay her rent. In the beginning of the film, Halley complained about losing her job as an exotic dancer for refusing to have sex with customers, so this decision on her part represents a decisive change in the arc of her character.

J. Brandon Colvin has argued that dorsality (as opposed to frontality) has been employed in art cinema as a stylistic choice to differentiate it from classical Hollywood cinema. Colvin claims that one of its functions is "denial of clear psychological/emotional access to characters."[75] Thus, when the shot of Halley appears, it is difficult to understand the motivation of the character. It is due not only to the camera position of the shot itself—denying the viewer access to her face—but also to the fact that only in retrospect can a viewer extrapolate its meaning, as well as the reason for the shot's placement within the sequence of scenes.

After Moonee takes a bath for a third time, Bobby observes a man leaving a woman's motel room. It is night and dark, so the viewer cannot be sure that it is Halley's room, but the hotel manager clearly seems concerned by what he has just witnessed. Bobby's suspicions are borne out when he asks Ashley directly whether she's been lending Halley rent money. The

phone call and the man's subsequent intrusion into the bathroom where Moonee is taking a bath provide an explanation
that an astute viewer might have guessed from the series of
vignettes. Halley, who earlier had refused to perform back-
room sex acts as an exotic dancer, has been forced to become
a prostitute as a last resort to keep Moonee and her afloat. The
revelation is a sad one, largely due to the fact that Moonee has
been exposed to it.

The next day, Halley and Moonee do dance moves as they
walk along the highway. After trying unsuccessfully to sell
four unused multicolored MagicBands (electronic tickets to
Disney World) at a Ticket Hut kiosk, Halley offers them to
a British tourist for $400. He purchases them after unsuc-
cessfully trying to bargain with her. Where did Halley get the
MagicBands to sell? Before we have time to ponder that question, Halley takes Moonee on a shopping spree, where they
spend the money on frivolous junk: gaudy trinkets, fake paper
money, and a bag of cotton balls. They act like two children:
Halley pushes Moonee around the gift store in a shopping cart.
She then skips across Route 192, still pushing Moonee in the
cart. Wearing pink paper angel wings, Halley turns up at the
lobby of the Magic Castle to pay the rent. Bobby asks, "Back in
the work force?" When Halley claims she is, Bobby tells her, "I
see you dressed in PJs all day, every day . . . If you're working,
who's looking after Moonee?"

The answer comes in the very next scene. From inside
Room 323, where Moonee and Halley lie on the bed, there is
a loud knock on the door. Halley gets up, looks through the
peephole, and yells loudly, "Go away, asshole, or I'm gonna
call the cops." As the guy bangs on the door and refuses to go
away, the commotion quickly brings Bobby, who attempts to

mediate. The angry guy (Macon Blair) demands that she return his four MagicBands.[76] Halley claims not to know him.
As the camera holds on a profile shot of Moonee, he insists
that Halley stole the MagicBands, which are worth $1,700,
out of his bag.

Bobby confronts the angry john who wants his stolen MagicBands back.

It suddenly becomes apparent to the viewer that he is the
john who walked into Halley's bathroom earlier. As the john
talks to Bobby, in the background Halley gives him the middle
finger and makes obscene gestures, simulating oral sex with
her tongue. Bobby suggests that he can call the cops and settle
the problem, but he reasons that the MagicBands must have
been for the guy's wife and kids. This effectively persuades
the john to drop the matter. After the john reluctantly leaves,
Halley tells Bobby, "It's about time you make yourself useful"
and slams the door. Inside, Moonee asks innocently, "Did he
have to pee again?"

After the john's car speeds off below, Bobby knocks on the
door and lays down new ground rules that any guests have to

check in first at the front office. He and Halley argue back and
forth. In a shot taken from inside the room, Bobby storms off.
Halley charges after him and follows him down the corridor
and the staircase. "You're not my father," she shouts at him.
She chases after him as he enters the lobby and yells, "Fuck
you, Bobby. I don't have to listen to you." Bobby demands that
she leave the lobby, threatens that he'll throw her out of the
motel, and begins counting. At the count of three, she rushes
out. After taking several brisk steps, she stops, reaches inside
her underwear, and returns to slap her bloody sanitary pad on
the glass door, while also giving him the middle finger.

Alexis Zabé considers this shot from a technical standpoint
to be the most difficult one in the entire film. The idea was
to shoot most of the scene in a single continuous take, but
part of it didn't work and two different takes had to be com-
bined through means of a jump cut in the editing. The shot
begins as Halley chases after Bobby and asks, "What the fuck
are you talking about?" As Bobby heads away from her in the
direction of the camera, the Steadicam moves backward as
Halley follows and argues with him for the entire length of
the balcony. As Bobby heads down the stairs, there is a jump
cut, and the camera follows Halley down the stairs as she pur-
sues him. The camera allows her to move in front of it as she
chases after Bobby, and it stays with her as she continues after
him into the motel lobby. The camera frames them in a shot
with Amber behind the desk and then in a two-shot as Bobby
counts to three. It then moves to frame Halley as she heads out
the door and then comes back to make a visual statement as
the camera frames the sanitary pad on the glass door and we
hear Bobby's response.

According to Zabé, rehearsing the complicated shot and

blocking and choreographing the movement of the actors took all day. In the shot, the camera had to track back as Halley chases after Bobby retreating along the long third-floor balcony, which meant their movements as well as the pacing of the dialogue had to be carefully coordinated. As the two of them argue, there is also another tenant sitting outside his room. When they pass by, he moves a green bottle next to his chair. The camera first follows Halley and then the two of them as they move down the stairs, which involved complicated movement on the different floor landings. A couple stands at one of the landings and Halley addresses the woman, which entailed precise timing. When Bobby enters the lobby on the ground floor, the camera has to frame Bobby, Amber, and finally Halley as she moves into the frame. As Bobby moves forward, the camera follows Halley's movement to include Bobby in the frame and then stays on her once she leaves. The complex process also involved keeping the actors in focus the whole time.

Attempting to cover a complicated scene involving movement in a single shot is technically very difficult. Zabé explains what it entailed: "We started out on the third floor on the Steadicam, walked all the way down the aisle [of the balcony], then walked three floors down stairs that go around, then came down and walked into the lobby, so we had the logistics of not seeing ourselves as we were going down the stairs."[77] In addition, the shot involved the full range of aperture openings on the lens due to the radical shifts in lighting—from a T-stop of 16 to wide open. The shot had to be done multiple times. Zabé estimates that they might have done as many as eleven different takes to get it right.

Moonee discusses the news media with Jancey as they stand under a tree in the rain before taking her on a safari.

The scene is intended to be another analog to Disney World—in this instance, the Kilimanjaro Safaris in Animal Kingdom. Moonee leads Jancey to an open field. Instead of elephants, giraffes, lions, zebras, and cheetahs, there is simply a small herd of cows, and the two children imitate the mooing sounds of the animals. This idyllic scene of childhood fun and fantasy, however, proves to be a lull before the storm. It presents a striking contrast to what follows. The film cuts to a night shot of Halley sauntering toward the camera and then knocking on Ashley's motel door. She can't understand why what happened with Moonee and Scooty should affect their relationship—"after all," she reasons, "they're kids." In one of her only vulnerable moments, Halley asks whether Ashley could spot her the rent this week. Ashley laughs and tells her, "I think you have that covered."

Ashley shows Halley a picture of her solicitation ad on her phone.

When Halley acts confused, Ashley informs her that everyone knows about her prostitution. She goes inside, gets her phone, and shows Halley the online photo that Moonee took of her mother in the bikini. Halley denies that the picture is of her. In disbelief, Ashley yells, "Those are your tats, bitch! Are you fucking kidding me? And I swear to God, if Scooty was ever in the room where you were whoring off, I'll fucking kill you!" Halley swiftly grabs Ashley by the head and pushes her into the room. From a shot behind Scooty, who sits on the bed in the foreground, Halley throws Ashley between the beds and pummels her multiple times with her fists. Halley then rushes downstairs to her own room, where she vomits in the toilet and puts her hands to her face and cries.

As we see in *Under the Rainbow*, the scene of Halley beating Ashley had to be performed with a stunt double because Mela Murder was three months pregnant at the time of the shooting. As a result, the violence happens away from the camera. What makes Halley's violence even more horrific is the fact that she is brutally punching Ashley in front of Scooty. (In Normal Mailer's *Maidstone* [1970], Mailer and actor Rip Torn got into an actual fight, a vicious one, on the set that made it into the film. Mailer's young children witnessed it, and Mailer never forgave Torn for assaulting him in front of his kids.) Placing the camera behind Scooty as he sits on the bed in the foreground had a twofold purpose. It allowed for the use of a stunt double to depict the violent beating, which was necessary in order to do the shot. But, secondly, the use of dorsality rather than frontality prevents us from seeing the impact this would have on Scooty, or on Christopher Rivera, the young actor who is playing him. Rivera was reassured that the violence he would be witnessing wasn't real by being shown the mechanics of the stunt beforehand.

The decision to place the camera behind Scooty puts the focus on him rather than the violence itself, which is also partially obscured by his head, the camera angle, and the fact that it's taking place behind the bed. The effect is to leave more to the imagination of the viewer. Alexis Zabé argues that withholding Scooty's facial reaction makes it more powerful: "To me it's much stronger and much more violent not to see his face and to just force you to get into his shoes in a way. Because once you see his face you become . . . a spectator to his anguish rather than becoming a spectator to the drama that is unfolding."[78] The fact that Scooty witnesses what has transpired is not ignored, because Halley glances overs at him before she leaves. In fact, her action is contained in the script: "Halley looks up and sees Scooty watching this, stunned and frozen. She leaves."[79]

The scene of Halley's violent assault comes as a shock. Up until now, she has only used her mouth as a weapon. Even when Bobby has tried to help her in a parental sort of way, she has rebuffed his kindness and concern, choosing instead to view him more as an authority figure—a role she can resent and one that he is uncomfortable playing. Even when Bobby comes to her defense at the Arabian Nights Motel, she doesn't appear at all grateful. Nor does she thank him when he manages to get rid of the john for her after she stole valuable MagicBands from him. Instead of gratitude, she suggests it is the least he could do for her. When they argue, flashing her bloody sanitary pad makes a crude statement, reinforced by a middle finger. It is her protest against a world that she struggles to navigate. But her assault of Ashley is telling. When faced with the truth of her actions, her response is outright denial. "That's not me," she protests to the utter astonishment of her former friend. But Ashley's threat regarding Scooty triggers her vicious attack because Halley knows it actually rings true for her own child, Moonee, given that the john inadvertently wandered into the bathroom.

It doesn't take long for there to be retribution. From the scene of Moonee and Jancey talking about recess on the seesaw, the film cuts to Bobby at his desk at the motel. When he happens to glance at the security camera, he notices two people standing outside Halley's motel room door. As Jancey talks about her grandmother, Moonee, riding the seesaw, stares offscreen while she bobs in and out of the frame. She tells her friend, "I think something's happening at my room." Bobby stands between two DCF agents in red shirts as Halley screams, "Did Ashley actually call the DCF on me?" When the agent will only say that they received a call, Halley shouts at the top of her lungs, "From who?" As Moonee and Jancey stand at the landing of the staircase, Bobby comes toward them. Moonee asks, "Why is my mom yelling?" Bobby discreetly gets Jancey to go back home. After asking Bobby more questions, Moonee suddenly shouts to her mom.

The film cuts to Jancey walking to Futureland and then back to Bobby and a DCF agent who sits on the staircase. Moonee asks, "Can I go back to my room now?" As Bobby tries to get her to answer the questions of the DCF agent, Moonee wraps her arms around her herself, pulls her legs in toward her body, lowers her head, and begins to rock back and forth slightly while refusing to speak. She turns her head away from the DCF agent, who asks, "Can you tell me what kinds of stuff you do every day, Moonee? Do you ever go swimming in the pool?" Moonee starts to nod her head in agreement but then appears to gesture "no" with a wave of her hand. Her conflicted response suggests that she might be about to cry.

Brooklynn Prince's performance in the scene is especially

noteworthy. It shows a side of her character we have not seen before. Up until now, viewers have mostly seen Moonee's bravado, which mimics that of Halley, but the hidden pathos of this young child suddenly begins to surface. Moonee clearly senses that her mother is in trouble with the authorities, which causes her to become anxious and upset. When asked about Prince's performance in the scene, Samantha Quan has an explanation for why the scene, even though it contains no dialogue, is so powerful. According to Quan, "Brooklynn was used to being sassy, but it wasn't working in the scene. The direction then became: You can't say any words, but you can use your body to say something to her [the DCF agent]."[80] The tension between Prince wanting to speak and not being able to speak translates into a subtle statement of her vulnerability. The young actor somehow succeeds in making us feel her internal conflict.

Moonee reacts to the DCF agent's questions.

Later, as Moonee sleeps in the bed, Halley is clearly upset. She stomps her foot on the floor. As Halley watches from the balcony in the rain, Ashley comes down the stairs on her way to work. They make eye contact. Halley and Moonee play together in the rain. They come back and begin to clean up the room in preparation for a visit from the DCF. Halley gives Bertha, who works in the laundry room, a large bag of weed.

The next morning, Halley takes Moonee to the Inn at Calypso Cay, one of the better hotels down Route 192. In a wide shot, the camera follows them as they walk holding hands and head in the direction of the lobby of the hotel. After a cut, a closer shot follows the two of them as they walk through the hallways toward the back of the dining room, where Moonee runs ahead to a food table. Baker only had time for a single take. As he explains, "*Everything* was wrong with it: You saw a mic pack on Bria, there was a big *Star Wars* poster in the lobby, there was a boom shadow, the Steadicam moved."[81] Using digital postproduction tools, including stabilization, Baker was able to clean up the shot and get it to work.

The ensuing breakfast buffet scene serves as a more obvious example of Baker's use of improvisation. Here is the scene as it appears in the script:

MOONEE: I wish forks were made of candy.
(beat)
Then I could eat the forks after my meal.
(beat)
We gotta come here all the time.
(beat)
Mom, you look busted.
(beat)
I'm going to put a strawberry, raspberry and bacon in my mouth at the same time.
(Moonee continues to stuff her face. A HOTEL WORKER [female, 20s] walks over, eyeing them.)
HOTEL WORKER: Could I get your room number?
HALLEY: 323.[82]

Prince's improvisation during the scene is infinitely better than what was scripted. Baker was offscreen feeding her lines to which she would then respond. Among the best are when Moonee says, "I love this." After Moonee gulps down a glass of orange juice in close-up, she continues, "I feel like I'm going to burp. I wish I had a bigger stomach . . . like I was pregnant. I'd fit food in that. . . . This is the life, man . . . better than a cruise. I mean there is not a cruise made out of all this food."

The film cuts from Halley staring lovingly at Moonee to a shot of Bobby, who has an anguished look on his face as he sits at the desk, presumably watching the security cameras offscreen. His name is called. The camera follows Halley as she walks up the stairs and along the length of the balcony toward her room. A frontal moving shot frames her as if she's slowly taking her final walk on death row, then closes on Moonee. The camera angle switches to a mobile shot behind them as Moonee asks, "Mom, what's going on?" Halley answers, "It's going to be okay, baby." Moonee replies, "What's going to be okay?"

The mobile camera alternates from in front and then behind as they approach Bobby, who is flanked by three DCF agents and two police officers waiting for Halley at her room. She walks past them defiantly and goes inside, asking, "You want to inspect my room? Be my guest." As a DCF investigator pulls Halley aside, the camera holds on a shot of Moonee, who listens intently as the investigator tells Halley, "We have security footage that shows nine different men entering and exiting your room over the last three weeks." Bobby interrupts in an attempt to shield Moonee from what's being said by asking whether she can go outside.

Bobby positions himself in the doorway so that he can

view both situations. An agent talks to Moonee, who appears confused, outside, while the film cuts back inside to where the investigator tells Halley, "We've also obtained this online classified ad soliciting customers for sexual activities with your phone number attached." One of the case workers talks to Moonee, suggesting that she'll have to go away but that it will only be "temporary." Moonee doesn't know what the word means.

Inside the room, the DCF investigator informs Halley that they are taking Moonee and have found a family in Polk County for her to stay with during the investigation. Moonee asks to say goodbye to Scooty. Bobby explains to the DCF officials that he lives downstairs in Room 223. Halley is told to pack a bag for Moonee. She does so but is clearly going through the motions. One of the DCF agents takes Moonee downstairs to say goodbye to Scooty. Ashley answers the door. Her face is badly bruised, causing Moonee to ask, "Ashley, what happened to your face?" Moonee gives Scooty an awkward hug and a high-five. As she's about to leave, Scooty blurts out, "My mom said you're going to another family." Afterward, Moonee asks the DCF worker, "Why did he say that I'm going to another family?"

As they head back upstairs, Moonee questions the workers about the fact that the police are taking her mother away. She becomes upset, as the film crosscuts among shots of Moonee, Halley, and Bobby. Moonee suddenly begins to resist. One of the DCF agents appeals to Halley for help. Incredulous, she asks, "You want me to help you take my child away? Are you retarded? You stupid, right?" As Moonee panics, Halley begins to throw a fit inside the room, causing the cops to rush inside. Moonee suddenly pushes past the DCF worker, who falls down the stairs chasing after her. The film cuts from Bobby's reaction to Moonee running in the motel parking lot. Moonee's flight causes Halley to become even more combative. As a helicopter flies overhead loudly, Moonee heads toward the Futureland Motel while everyone else panics. When Halley realizes that Moonee has run off, she yells, "You let her just run away? And I'm the one who's unfit?" Halley moves closer to the camera, so that her mouth appears in an extremely tight close-up, and screeches, "Fuck you!"

Moonee frantically knocks on the door of Jancey's motel room. Jancey looks out from behind the curtain of the window. Baker cuts from Grandma Stacy, who is serving lunch to Jancey's younger sister, Luci, to Moonee at the door. Jancey asks, "Moonee, what's wrong?" From a shot of Grandma Stacy and Luci, who has spilled her bowl of food, the film cuts back to the door where Moonee stands near tears and says, "Please." Jancey responds, "You're scaring me." Moonee tells her, "You're my best friend, and this may be the only time I ever see you again." Jancey asks, "What's going on?" Moonee begins to cry big tears that cover her entire flushed face. Moonee tells her, "I can't say it."

Jancey shows concern for her friend Moonee.

Jancey and Moonee flee toward Disney World.

The camera holds on Grandma Stacy's face as she looks up and hears the sound of Moonee crying at the door. Moonee puts her fingers in her mouth as tears continue to roll down her cheeks. Jancey looks at Moonee and begins to breathe very heavily, as if to cry. She suddenly reaches and takes Moonee's hand and leads her away, as the music changes into an orchestral rendition of "Celebration" and the image changes from 35 mm to digital video shot on an iPhone 6s. The two girls head past the Giant Mermaid and Lighthouse Gift Shop and down the highway, across green fields, and through the parking lot toward Disney World.[83] As they disappear inside, the camera tracks after them. They head straight through a crowd toward Cinderella Castle, creating an ambiguous ending that suddenly blurs the line between harsh reality and fantasy that lies at the heart of the story.

Reception

REALITY OR FANTASY

The original ending of the June 27 shooting script was for Moonee to flee alone. The new ending had Moonee and Jancey escaping into Disney World, to the Magic Kingdom, but initially it was intended that they would continue to Tomorrowland, where they would ride the Astro Orbiter and fly off to the moon together. Bergoch even shot a sample video of the ride in order to illustrate to Baker what he had in mind. The Astro Orbiter consists of little rockets that lift off and spin around in a circle, much like a carnival ride.

Baker was never sold on the idea of the Astro Orbiter for the ending. He and his crew nevertheless took the child actors to Disney World during production in order to shoot tests of them on the ride. Valeria Cotto, however, found the Astro Orbiter to be very scary. She immediately started to cry, and Brooklynn Prince followed suit. Even after being allowed to go on their favorite attraction, the Voyage of the Little Mermaid, it became obvious that the child actors still wanted no part of the Astro Orbiter, so the idea had to be scrapped.

Bergoch, who was enamored with the space theme, was initially distraught over this development, but Baker became convinced that the ending would still work if the two children simply headed toward the Magic Kingdom. In fact, he

Brooklynn Prince and Valeria Cotto on the Astro Orbiter ride at Disney World. Photo courtesy of Marc Schmidt.

thought it actually worked much better. In the final draft of the screenplay, the Astro Orbiter ride has been eliminated, and it is Jancey, in fact, who leads Moonee toward the castle:

EXT. VARIOUS ROUTE 192 LOCATIONS—DAY
Jancey leads Moonee off the beaten path, eventually toward a phone line in the shape of a certain mouse.
     Jancey and Moonee make their way to Route 535 and then Route 14 leading to the Magic Kingdom.

EXT. ENTRANCE SIGN—DAY
Jancey continues to lead Moonee toward the entrance sign of the THEME PARK property at an even faster pace.

EXT. THEME PARK ENTRANCE GATES—DAY
Jancey encourages Moonee to hurry up and follow her
toward a big parking lot entrance gate. A MONORAIL
whizzes by overhead.

EXT. THEME PARK—MAIN STREET—DAY
Jancey and Moonee's little torn-up sneakers run past
hundreds of tourists' legs, park maps and deflated balloons on the asphalt of the park's "Main Street USA."

　　Moonee's feet pick up speed. She hops over a spilled
MOUSESHAPED ICE CREAM BAR. Her feet leap out
of frame.

EXT. THEME PARK—DAY
Jancey and Moonee sprint faster than ever...

　　Weaving through TOURISTS... through CAST
MEMBERS...

　　They race toward a perfect enchanted storybook
CASTLE, glimmering in the sun against a dreamlike sky.[1]

Bergoch now agrees with the decision about the ending. As
he puts it, "Beyond Cinderella Castle is Fantasyland, so chaos
led us to a better ending after all."[2] Bergoch might not have
gotten the ending he wanted, but he did suggest the idea
of using an orchestral version of "Celebration," the song that
opens the film. According to Baker, the idea came during the
editing of the film:

　　We didn't script that, and then in post-production—I
　　edit consecutively, in order, almost like a fine cut, I don't
　　even do a rough cut or an assemble, I go right in—and
　　we were months into the edit and getting to the end, and
　　he was like, "Did you ever consider doing an orchestrated

'Celebration' at the end?" and I was like, "thank you!" because first I thought I was going to be doing some sort of
sound-scape-y sounds of the park and laughter.[3]

The addition of the song to the film's ending adds a trium-
phant note that, as much as anything, contributes to the
scene's uplifting quality.

The ending of the film was always supposed to take place
in Disney World, but this created obvious logistical problems
for the filmmakers. The Walt Disney Company is known to be
a litigious company and is notorious for enforcing its intellec-
tual property. There was no question that if the production
sought permission to shoot inside the theme park, it would
never be granted. The depiction of the hidden homeless right
on the doorstep of Disney World almost certainly would not
have been viewed favorably by a company that refers to all its
employees as "cast members" in the creation of a fantasy world
aimed at children.

The production scouted Universal Studios as a possible alternative location and even considered trying to recreate the
gates of Disney World and perhaps shoot a ride at a different
amusement park. But, in the end, there was simply no getting
around it—the production needed to shoot in the location.
Luckily, there was another precedent. Randy Moore had used a
Canon 5D Mark II (which looks very much like a still camera)
and succeeded in secretly shooting his independent film *Escape from Tomorrow* at both Disney theme parks without obtaining permits or permission from the Walt Disney Company.

Produced under great secrecy, Moore's film premiered at the
2013 Sundance Film Festival. In his review of the film, Matt
Zoller Seitz writes, "'Escape from Tomorrow' is an act of cultural vandalism, the feature film equivalent of drawing genitals

on cute storybook animals."[4] Disney chose to ignore the film rather than take legal action to suppress it. Seitz speculates:

> Maybe Disney's lawyers realized it's not appropriate to try to silence a comedy because it dares to treat Disney World and its copyrighted rides and characters as one might treat any other iconic site that families visit, such as the Washington mall or Times Square. To insist otherwise might have invited a legal battle—one that Disney would have lost, once the jury realized that "Escape from Tomorrow" was a political as well as an artistic statement, and that the decision to shoot on location was essential to its mood and message.[5]

Whatever the Walt Disney Company's reasons for not taking legal action against the film, there is no question that doing so would have called greater attention to it. Perhaps the notoriety of the case would have backfired against the Walt Disney Company in the long run, so that might have been a calculation on the part of the entertainment company.

Given its abject subject matter, *The Florida Project* no doubt would have created even more negative publicity than a recently fired businessman's paranoid visions within the amusement park, which was the subject of *Escape from Tomorrow*. A legal case over Baker's film might have called greater media attention to the stark juxtaposition of homeless kids living in motels nearby and a company whose CEO, Bob Iger, made nearly $66 million a year, or "about 1,424 times a Disney employee's median pay."[6]

Before stepping down as CEO on February 25, 2020, Iger had been under attack by Walt Disney's granddaughter, Abigail Disney, for paying such low wages when his own salary was so inflated. After receiving a complaint from a "cast member," she met with a number of Disney employees in July 2019. The Disney family member responded, "Every single one of these people I talked to were saying, 'I don't know how I can maintain this face of joy and warmth when I have to go home and forage for food in other people's garbage.'"[7]

As a precaution, the producers of *The Florida Project* consulted with lawyers Michael C. Donaldson and Lisa A. Callif, authors of the book *Clearance & Copyright*, who had advised on the theatrical release of *Escape from Tomorrow*, which was released through Cinetic Media's small distribution wing PDA (Producers Distribution Agency). Producers Chinoy and Silvestri reviewed the detailed legal arguments that were made by lawyers as a condition of Moore's film receiving errors and omissions insurance, which protects the distributor in the event of a lawsuit. The financial stakes were much higher for *The Florida Project* than for *Escape from Tomorrow* due to its larger budget. According to Chinoy, Callif was the lawyer who mostly worked with them in obtaining the E&O insurance necessary to be able to shoot at Disney World.[8]

The producers of *The Florida Project* were encouraged by the fact that the Walt Disney Company did not take legal action against *Escape from Tomorrow*, which was a far more egregious example of infringement than Baker's proposed ending. Ultimately, the producers on *The Florida Project* decided that it could easily be shot on an iPhone and, more importantly, that it was worth the legal risks involved. *Escape from Tomorrow* and *The Florida Project* are not the only two indie films willing to take risks by claiming "fair use." Josh and Benny Safdie adopted a similar stance on their recent film *Uncut Gems* (2019). According to Kelefa Sannch in the *New Yorker*, "The brothers used N.B.A. footage without permission, and are planning to offer a 'fair use' defense if the league objects; to strengthen their hypothetical case, they present the games exactly as they occurred, taking no license with the outcomes or the chronology."[9]

Obtaining the final shot clandestinely within the confines of Disney World, however, was by no means easy. Alexis Zabé, the cinematographer, claims the shot was challenging for a number of reasons. He indicates, for instance, that "the iPhone is a hard camera to use—it does what it wants."[10] Baker originally wanted to do the shot in a single take, but he underestimated the difficulty and gave up on the idea. Due to the complexity of having to move the child actors and camera a great distance through the unsuspecting "guests" at the theme park, the final shot wound up having to be done numerous times over two separate days. It was cloudy and rainy the first day, according to Alex Coco, and "the shot of the castle wasn't as gorgeous as Sean had hoped."[11] When Zabé finally was able to get a usable shot with the iPhone 6s, it was still not perfect—the sky had to be corrected in postproduction.

The last shot had to be carefully planned, and crew had to be reduced to a minimum. The group consisted of Baker, Zabé, Coco, Samantha Quan, Kevin Chinoy, Chris Bergoch, and the production stills photographer, Marc Schmidt, who was there for the first shoot. According to Coco, "Everyone's jobs are pretty obvious, but my job was to keep the iPhones cool (in a lunchbox filled with ice packs) so they didn't overheat and stop working (it was Florida in August), also keeping the batteries charged, the lenses clean and handing Alexis a new one when he wanted (we had two that rotated after every few takes)."[12]

In addition, the crew had to attempt to blend in with the other "guests" at the theme park that day. They were disguised as a family visiting Disney World for the first time. They all donned blue shirts that read "Thaler Family Magical Summer Vacation The Orlando Chronicles: WDW 1st Visit!" Coco designed them in photoshop with Chris Bergoch.[13]

The ending of *The Florida Project* is a tour de force for two reasons. First, Brooklynn Prince's performance in the scene where Moonee cries as she says goodbye to her best friend, Jancey, turns out to be a key element in creating a deep emotional impact on viewers. The second factor is the abrupt tonal switch, which catches viewers completely off guard. The threat of Moonee being separated from her mother by the DCF will surely seal the family's doom, yet the unexpected happens when Jancey suddenly grabs Moonee's hand, the orchestral version of "Celebration" plays, and the two children escape to Disney World and head toward Cinderella Castle. It has a buoyant, exhilarating effect on most viewers, who want the world to be better than that place of homeless motels full of people with no hope and children with no futures—even if it represents only a momentary respite, which is after all the function of happy endings in films.

Location and scheduling dictated that Moonee's dramatic crying scene be shot early in the production schedule. Such

Jancey and Moonee head toward Cinderella Castle.

scenes are usually saved for the end of a production, when the performers and crew are more fully functioning as a coherent team. Baker was extremely upset that he was forced for practical and budgetary reasons to stage the scene so early. No one had any idea whether Brooklynn Prince would be able to cry. Prince was very nervous about having to perform in the scene. She talked about it constantly on set and tried to put it off for as long as possible.

According to Samantha Quan, Prince is "great at 'what ifs.'" Quan was there on set and able to communicate with the young actor during the scene where she cries. She explains, "Brooklynn has an amazing ability to immerse herself into the circumstances of a situation. This was a scene that we could share with her the reality of the scene (unlike ones where the circumstances were too delicate for her to know)."[14] The scene was done in one long take. According to Kevin Chinoy, "Sean didn't stop bugging me for three days until he knew that the film had been processed and digitized and he had it."[15]

Baker admits that he had no idea whether Prince would be able to pull off such an emotionally demanding scene, even though the film was dependent on it. Baker told Amy Taubin for *Film Comment*, "I remember looking at my acting coach and cinematographer, and we were all teary-eyed. We were shooting in 35 mm, so we had to send the film to Atlanta to get processed and to New York to get scanned. I was so nervous. But when I called New York, they said you have 50-year-old guys in the transfer room crying."[16] Baker was ecstatic. Knowing he already had filmed the most difficult scene gave him enormous confidence that the film would be something special, even during the times when it looked as if the entire production might fall apart for a host of other reasons.

In *Under the Rainbow*, it is possible to watch the actual filming of the scene. We see Prince's face on the monitor. What is particularly striking is Brooklynn Prince's professionalism. She appears to understand what is at stake for her as a performer, and she remains very focused on the task at hand. She and Cotto would often fool around before filming a scene, but as she prepares to perform the crying scene, Prince tells her fellow actor, "Valeria, don't talk to me, okay? I'm trying to think of things sad so I can cry, okay?" She tells Baker, whose head is in the foreground, "I'm trying . . . I'm trying to cry."

Cotto's head is in the foreground of the shot as the camera frames Prince closely. Baker shouts, "Action!" As Prince breathes heavily, Baker tells Prince, "Look back at her." Baker adds, "You're scared!" He says, "Please hurry." Prince repeats the line. Baker and Quan both say, "Reach out to her." Prince is suddenly confused and unsure what to do next. Baker calmly directs her to "reach to her [Valeria's] shoulder." Prince touches Cotto's shoulder and then, rather astonishingly and without missing a beat, continues to deliver her lines. Prince says, "Please," and suddenly begins to cry.

Moonee breaks down and cries as she says goodbye to Jancey.

Prince hesitates for a moment. In a high-pitched child's voice, Baker feeds her the line, "You're my best friend, please." Still crying, Prince says, "You're my best friend . . . and I'm never going to see you again." Baker, who appears very excited but under great pressure, instructs her to say "goodbye" to her friend. With her hand in her mouth and still crying, Prince says, "Goodbye!" She extends the second syllable of the word and suddenly breaks down and begins to sob. Baker points frantically with his finger and tells her to exit screen right. As she does, Baker and Quan rush toward the child actor. Quan sweeps Prince up into her arms as the child actor continues to cry uncontrollably. Quan tells her afterward, "You're so brave." Prince calls her mother and tells her, "Mr. Sean says I'm the best actor he's ever met." Quan adds, "In his whole life." Prince repeats this additional information to her mother.

Is the ending real, or is it simply a child's fantasy? Many viewers and critics seem divided on this issue. Even Baker and Bergoch hold different views. For some, like Bergoch, the ending could have a literal interpretation, or it could be a fantasy:

> It's the ultimate leave-it-up-to-you ending, but I would like to think it's exactly what you're seeing. I think Jancey is a hero, and Jancey is saving the day there with what she thinks is the right move. It's like the classic *Wizard of Oz* ending—I thought Dorothy really did go to Oz, others say it was all a dream. The truth is I don't know what happens. I just know that Jancey is stepping up and becoming a true friend for her friend in need.[17]

Baker loves the ambiguous ending to his film because it's open to many different points of view and analyses, but he nonetheless interprets it as a dream sequence, a fantasy moment, and a "moment of escape":

> Unfortunately, I feel the film does end when she says goodbye and DCF shows up and the cops show up and find her seconds later when she says goodbye to Jancey. But we take the audience on that last hopeful journey the way that the kids have used their imagination throughout the whole film. They finally reach that place that they always wanted to go, but couldn't go—a place inhabited by people that don't even know they exist.[18]

Whether real or fantasy, the ending of the film proved highly divisive.

The ending also drew comment by nearly every critic in reviews of the film. Michael Koretsky in *Reverse Shot* suggests that the ending, which reinforces the tension between "authenticity" and "delusion" could be divisive to viewers, "as it comes across as facile, or at least too simple, a final refuge for characters already given no past or future. As it should be, it's left up to the viewer to decide what to make of Moonee and Halley and what will happen to them once they escape the camera's curious eye."[19]

David Rooney in the *Hollywood Reporter* found it "abrupt" yet "tender." He writes, "Baker captures their possibly imaginary flight together to a magical destination via a brief burst of guerilla-style filming. And that stylistic switch is as much a part of the director's content-dictated aesthetic as the limpid compositions and singing colors that infuse this movie about low-rent lives with such visual richness."[20]

Corey Atad in *Slate* considers the ending to be "as perfect an ending as has graced the screen in years." For this critic, the ending was unexpected, risky, and highly complex, and represented a complete shift from what came before, comparable to that of F. W. Murnau's *The Last Laugh* (1924): "For one breathless minute the lives of these children take on all the magic promised by the Magic Kingdom. It's the granting of a wish, made possible by hope, and love, and friendship, and the sympathies of a filmmaker, though the knowledge of the harsher reality waiting for them never dissipates. Happiness and heartbreak exist at once. It's the entire film in microcosm, and then it's over."[21] The suggestion is that the ending causes viewers to experience seemingly conflicting emotions simultaneously, which is partly why viewers might hold such differing views.

The reviewer for *BuzzFeed News*, Anne Helen Petersen, found the ending to be provocative:

> The film doesn't have a happy ending, but it's not maudlin. Instead, it's a provocative depiction of the realities of postrecession America, highlighting the fragility and necessity of the fantasies that buoy us just above the surface. The uneasiness that comes from the film—that bittersweetness that sticks in your throat—stems from the way Baker communicates something we've known, and forced ourselves to forget, about how people live in this country. It's a slice of life smashed right in your face.[22]

The reviewer's last sentence suggests the political power of what Sean Baker achieves in *The Florida Project* by refusing to sugarcoat his message.

Equally controversial to viewers is the film's depiction of the character Halley. Many viewers found her to be harsh and abrasive, and, hence, ultimately unsympathetic. Some people view her as an irresponsible parent. Robert Koehler, for instance, was quoted in *Cineaste* describing her as "monstrous" and "someone who can safely be termed the most horrific parent put up on screen in recent memory (including the awful parents in *It*)."[23] Although she tries to find a job, Halley does drugs, cons and steals, and eventually prostitutes herself. She also becomes savagely violent in her physical attack on Ashley, which provokes retribution from her former friend.

Baker and Bergoch, who wrote the character, were not trying to make Halley likeable or endearing to audiences. Instead, they wanted to create a truthful depiction of a single mother who might find herself in such a dire situation. In interviews, Baker has defended Halley as a character. For him, to dislike her for her behavior amounts to a case of blaming the victim: "Audiences should, at the very least, consider this character's situation—having Moonee at fifteen years old, no education, no family support. Who knows where Moonee's father is? Halley's unemployable, she has no options. I don't care if you think she has a dirty mouth, or is rebellious. But I'd like audiences to have empathy for her."[24]

"Stigma" is a word that Baker often uses in defending his characters, especially those who are sex workers. But the word could also apply to the entire community of the hidden homeless, who also bear a stigma. "Removing the stigma," he told *Collider*, "is the most important through line in my work; removing the stigma from hopelessness, removing the stigma from sex work, what my movies do is put a human face and help people perceive these stigmatized professions and communities in a much different way. I think that's the ultimate goal with these films."[25]

In his book *Stigma*, Erving Goffman postulates that

"normal" people view a person with a stigma "as not quite human." He adds, "On this assumption we exercise varieties of discrimination, through which we effectively, if often unthinkingly, reduce his life chances. We construct a stigma-theory, an ideology to explain his inferiority and account for the danger he represents, sometimes rationalizing an animosity based on other differences, such as those of social class."[26]

The Reverend Mary Lee Downey, the head of Hope 192, talks about the homeless essentially living in a perpetual survival mode. Her position is similar to that of Baker. Speaking of the homeless, she observes, "They don't make the best choices from a middle-class perspective. We put the onus on them, but if we had higher wages, affordable housing, support for single moms, maybe they wouldn't be in the situation."[27] Halley certainly fits into that category, and Baker is trying to be true to this type of flawed character. As he puts it, "I've seen many films about the mom/daughter relationship and hookers with hearts of gold. But the films that don't work for me are the ones that sanctify these characters and make them saints that aren't even human. I can't believe them or connect with them in any way."[28]

Halley is someone who is desperately trying to keep things together but aware that she's losing the battle. She is not at all mean to her daughter—quite the opposite. If she has any redeeming qualities, it is that she loves Moonee more than anything in the world, which is why she is willing to do whatever is necessary to provide for her within the rather desperate circumstances in which they find themselves. The scene where she takes her sanitary pad from inside her underwear and slaps it on the window when arguing with Bobby is the kind of in-your-face vulgar gesture that is bound to repulse certain viewers. Even Vinaite wasn't sure she would be able to do such a thing on camera. But her gesture is actually a form of visceral protest against her plight.

If Halley is controversial as a character, Vinaite's performance also managed to polarize critics and viewers. Rooney in the *Hollywood Reporter* seems most critical of her performance in his review, citing the limits of using nonprofessional actors: "Vinaite lacks the nuance as an actor to make the pathos real, so her screaming rants and destructive explosions tend to come off like the playacting tantrums of reality TV. Unskilled kids can get away with a lot on-camera, because in a sense they're always performing, plus Baker has found disarming naturals. But too often, Vinaite's self-consciousness shows."[29]

Rooney's assessment is atypical. Owen Gleiberman in *Variety* praises the acting of not only Brooklynn Prince and Willem Dafoe but Bria Vinaite as well, finding her raw and gritty performance to be not just remarkable but central to the film:

> Yet it would be a righteous good thing if all the attention won by Prince and Dafoe didn't overshadow the *other* remarkable performance in "The Florida Project"—the one that, more than any other, defines the film. That's the work of Bria Vinaite as Halley, Moonee's loving, raging, and desperately dysfunctional mother, whose slow but sure voyage along the path to self-sabotage forms the explosive core of the movie.[30]

Gleiberman expands on the schizoid effect that her character has on viewers by suggesting that we hold conflicting responses to her: "What we're really watching is the study of a charismatic but pathological personality, and the most haunting aspect of 'The Florida Project' is the burn of reality that

Vinaite brings to the role." Calling her a "true anti-heroine," he adds, "You could argue that she's the film's central figure, a mother struggling to do right by her child, but you could also say that she's its principal monster. That's the harrowing beauty—the journey—of 'The Florida Project': the way that we're for her and against her at the same time."[31]

CRITICAL RESPONSE

The Florida Project premiered at the Directors Fortnight at the 2017 Cannes Film Festival. It generated interest from three major distributors: Amazon, Neon, and A24. It was picked up by A24, the distributor of Barry Jenkins's *Moonlight*, and was considered the "hot buy" at Cannes. Anne Thompson observed in *IndieWire* at the time, "A24 could look to achieve what Fox Searchlight managed with 2012 indie breakout 'Beasts of the Southern Wild,' which debuted in Sundance and went on to ride strong Cannes buzz and the fall festival circuit to four nominations, including Best Picture, Writer, Director, and its nine-year-old star, Quvenzhané Wallis, who became the youngest-ever nominee for Best Actress."[32]

The film also had its US premiere at the New York Film Festival in October and garnered numerous critical accolades. *The Florida Project* was the runner-up for Best Picture from the Los Angeles Film Critics Association, finishing behind *Call Me by Your Name* (2017). Willem Dafoe received the Best Supporting Actor award. He also received the same award from the New York Film Critics Circle, while Sean Baker won the Best Director award. Baker was also nominated for Best Director and *The Florida Project* for Best Picture by the Indie Spirit Awards. The film also won the Best Film award from the AFI.

There was a great deal of Oscar excitement surrounding the film. It was expected to receive nominations in several categories: Best Picture, Best Director, Best Actress, and Best Supporting Actor, as well as possibly Best Screenplay and Best Cinematography. Yet, when the Academy Award nominations were announced, *The Florida Project* received only one: Willem Dafoe for Best Supporting Actor.

Esquire saw the snub as an indication that Hollywood hadn't really changed. Although a film about women, *Lady Bird* (2017), and another involving gay subject matter, *Call Me by Your Name*, were nominated, Olivia Ovenden calls overlooking *The Florida Project* for a number of award nominations "the Academy's big misstep this year."[33] She continues, "But somehow, *The Florida Project*'s poignant exploration of white American poverty and the hidden homeless has been deemed less worthy—despite, one might argue, a recent election that showed the urgent need for America's poor and downtrodden to be heard."[34]

Ovenden lamented the Academy passing over Bria Vinaite and Brooklynn Prince for Best Actress nominations, but considered it even more confounding that the Academy ignored Sean Baker's achievement in directing the film: "But perhaps the biggest shock is that Baker himself was not nominated for Best Director. After all, he won the New York Film Critics Circle Award for *The Florida Project*—the same prize which started Barry Jenkins' trajectory to multiple wins for *Moonlight*."[35] Citing his "bold and visionary ending" as proof that Baker was striving for something different and unconventional, she writes,

His direction shrinks your worldview into that of a child: ice-cream stands tower over you, a paddock of stray

horses [cows] becomes a safari and watching the Disney
World fireworks from the outskirts of the park really is
magical. It is a world full of people that are all tipped over
but, somehow, still growing. It would be a crying shame
if less people see it because the Academy could not.[36]

Even Dafoe, who received the only nomination, for Best Supporting Actor, expressed disappointment that *The Florida
Project* was overlooked in other categories, especially Baker
for Best Director, because "this is very much his movie and he
made a beautiful movie."[37]

Newsweek was even more blunt in its assessment. The head-
line for an article after Oscar nominations were announced de-
clared that *The Florida Project* was "robbed." The writer, Mary
Kaye Schilling, believed that Brooklynn Prince deserved a nomination for Best Actress. She argues, "Her performance is one
of those once-in-a-generation star-making turns that knocks
you flat. Yet she was shut out at the Oscars."[38] Schilling felt
The Florida Project deserved two other nominations: one for
Best Original Screenplay and a second one for Alexis Zabé for
Best Cinematography. Like *Esquire's*, the *Newsweek* writer was
concerned about the social effect of Baker's film not getting the
nominations it deserved. Schilling writes, "It's both the most
devastating and euphoric film experience of 2017. A few more
Oscar nominations would have encouraged people to see it."[39]

Paste also decried the fact that *The Florida Project* did not
receive a Best Picture nomination and called it "this year's
Oscar travesty."[40] Scott Russell, the reviewer, echoes *Newsweek*
in indicating that the film should have received other award
nominations as well. He writes, "Ultimately, *The Florida Project*
deserves more than just the Supporting Actor nod it received

and the Best Picture nomination it didn't. There are arguments to be made for Baker's direction, for Zabé's cinematography, for Prince and Vinaite's performances. Above all, like the people it portrays, *The Florida Project* deserves to be seen, felt, appreciated and discussed."[41] For Baker, the Oscar snub likewise meant that fewer people would be exposed to the social issue of the hidden homeless. He also felt sorry for his actors, namely Bria Vinaite and Brooklynn Prince, because "the recognition they would have gotten would have changed their lives."[42]

Those outraged reviewers were right about the lack of Oscar nominations for *The Florida Project* having a negative impact at the box office. Although the film was a critical success, it ended up grossing only $5.9 million domestically and almost $11 million worldwide. Although that is respectable for an independent film with only one big-name performer, it would have gotten a major boost from more nominations and would have been seen by more people. As of this writing, the film has a rating of 96 percent on the movie aggregator site Rotten Tomatoes and 92 percent on Metacritic.

Why didn't *The Florida Project* receive more Oscar nominations? Although the answer will always remain a mystery, there are a number of theories. For one thing, the film, by design, did not have recognizable stars other than Willem Dafoe, whose performance did get recognized. On the other hand, Bria Vinaite, Mela Murder, and Brooklynn Prince were virtually unknown to Academy voters, no matter how strong their performances, which can work against a film's chances for Oscar nominations. The film's abject subject matter, unconventional structure, and documentary-like social realism could have been factors—it was perceived as an "indie" film by the industry.

The Oscars, as Shih-Ching Tsou notes, are "very political."[43] She argues that Oscar nominations are all about the campaigns and how much money distributors are willing to put into them. She explains, "I understand why Oscar films are Oscar films. It's all about those campaigns. They spend a lot of money inviting important people to go to the screenings and expensive parties."[44] The film's distributor, A24, also had another of its films in contention, Greta Gerwig's *Lady Bird*, which might also have been a factor.

In contrast to *The Florida Project, Lady Bird* is a more conventional comedy, by a female director, with a cast of recognizable actors that includes Saoirse Ronan, Laurie Metcalf, Lucas Hedges, and Timothée Chalamet. The film grossed nearly $49 million in domestic release and almost $79 million worldwide, so it did substantially better at the box office. This might have convinced A24 to put a great deal more money into the Oscar campaign for *Lady Bird* than into that of *The Florida Project. Lady Bird* ended up receiving five nominations, including Best Picture, Best Director, Best Original Screenplay, Best Female Actor (Saoirse Ronan), and Best Female Actor in a Supporting Role (Laurie Metcalf). It did not win in any of the categories.

Despite the snub by the Academy, reviews of *The Florida Project* were at times ecstatic. Justin Chang, the critic for the *Los Angeles Times*, wrote of the film, "Scene by scene, it assembles one of the most infectious and thrillingly alive portraits of childhood I've ever seen." He adds, "In its final moments 'The Florida Project' makes an astonishing, lyrical leap, one that confirms my sense that Baker is not just an unusually observant filmmaker but also a full-fledged magician, a practitioner of the sublime. He has ventured into a world that few of us know and emerged with a masterpiece of empathy and imagination."[45] The reviewer for *BuzzFeed News* writes, "*The Florida Project* isn't just one of the best, most provocative, and most beautiful films of the year: It's proof that indie cinema's resonance in the cultural mainstream didn't end with Weinstein, and that there's still room for weird, incredibly *filmic* narratives that resist basically all Hollywood formulas—and not just on streaming platforms."[46]

The film wound up on a number of top-ten lists for best films of the year, including aggregate critic polls at *IndieWire*, *Sight & Sound*, and the *Village Voice*. *The Florida Project* made the best-film lists of both Manohla Dargis and A. O. Scott of the *New York Times*. Scott, in fact, picked it as his number one film of the year:

> The promise of an independent, socially conscious, aesthetically adventurous homegrown cinema is spectacularly redeemed in Sean Baker's latest feature, which managed to be both the most joyful and the most heartbreaking movie of the year. Steeped in the gaudy materialism of Central Florida, animated by Brooklynn Prince's gleeful spontaneity and anchored by Willem Dafoe's deep craft, the movie already has a feeling of permanence. Ms. Prince's Moonee has earned a place in the canon of American mischief alongside the likes of Eloise and Tom Sawyer.[47]

Such critical praise of the film did make the Academy's choices seem rather myopic, especially when nine films received Oscar nominations for Best Picture that year, while Baker's film was somehow overlooked.

Despite being virtually ignored at the Oscars, *The Florida Project* did manage to bring significant public attention to the issue of the hidden homeless. The distributor donated a small portion of digital sales of the film to the Community Hope Center in Kissimmee to aid in their mission to help the homeless in the area.

In addition, the critical success of the film affected the various nonprofessional cast members, including the child actors. *The Florida Project* brought a great amount of media attention to Bria Vinaite. Profiles of her appeared in *Vanity Fair*, *W* magazine, *IndieWire*, and the *Independent*. She went on a four-month press tour with the film, did photo shoots as a model, and had a cameo in a music video by the well-known rapper Drake. Her role as Halley, in effect, launched her acting career within the industry. Of course, because the role she was playing in *The Florida Project* had a certain authenticity related to her as a person, Vinaite resented finding herself being typecast. She told one interviewer,

> People only see me as Halley, and I almost feel like now I'm at a point where I have to prove to everyone that that's not all I can do. People assume that I'm this trashy motel girl, and that those are the only roles I can play, but I really take it seriously, and I know that I can do more. I want to do comedy, I want to do horror, I want to do all these other things. But that's why I think it's super important for me to create things rather than just act.[48]

Vinaite is now represented by Thirty Three Management. She appeared in Jamie Simon's British-American film *Balance, Not Symmetry* (2019) and made a guest appearance in two episodes of *The OA*, season 2 (2019), but so far she has not been able to capitalize on the success of her debut role.

Baker has made it a point to introduce first-time actors or

new talent to the industry, but their breakout success is often short-lived given the cutthroat nature of the industry, where newfound success can easily become the "flavor of the week." Baker makes sure to warn his first-time actors of the pitfalls. Neither Prince Adu nor Karren Karagulian, for instance, found success following their appearances in Baker films, although trans star Mya Taylor from *Tangerine* was able to land a spot as a recurring character on the major TV series *Dietland* (2018).

The same has been true for some of the first-time actors in the films of the Safdie brothers. In the *New Yorker* profile on the Safdies, Kelefa Sanneh describes the fact that Arielle Holmes appeared to be a rising star in the industry following her breakout performance in *Heaven Knows What* but ended up fading quickly. Buddy Duress, who was on the run from the police during the shooting of the same film, spent a year in prison afterward. He rebounded and resurfaced in major roles in such films as the Safdies' *Good Time* and Dustin Guy Defa's *Person to Person* (2017), but he "ended up in jail on drug charges."[49] According to Josh Safdie, "He was doing so well. And he just got sucked back into that world."[50]

Baker observes, "For me, Spike Lee was always one that really did it right. He would have big A-list stars in his films, and then he would always give fresh faces to some of the bigger supporting characters. He would be introducing so many new faces to the world, new talent to the industry, which is I think really important."[51] It is not a minor issue for Baker, who is always inclined to cast first-time actors in his films, but rather a deliberate part of the politics of how he is attempting to transform the industry in which he works.

The child actors became minor celebrities once the film was released. They have Twitter accounts and gave interviews to *IndieWire*. Brooklynn Prince appeared on *Jimmy Kimmel Live!*, where he managed to get her to give everyone the middle finger—a gesture she made in the film. Prince had a role in *The Lego Movie 2: The Second Part* (2018) and did voice work in *The Angry Birds Movie 2* (2019). She also directed a short movie, entitled *Colours* (2019), with some assistance from Sean Baker. Most recently, Prince had a starring role in the gothic horror film *The Turning* (2020) from Universal Pictures and a headlining role in the Apple TV series *Home Before Dark* (2020–), signaling that the industry has recognized her considerable talent.

When Jennifer Conrader of CROWDshot read the scriptment for *The Florida Project* in April 2016, she did have one major concern. She asked Baker, "What's the purpose of this film?" She wondered whether they were going to make a film about homeless kids in Florida and then simply leave. Baker, however, convinced her that he wanted to use his storytelling skills to get people to act. She ultimately felt that he delivered on that promise.[52]

The biggest success the film may have achieved is that Christopher Rivera, who played the good-natured Scooty, ended up being offered a college scholarship by Rollins College in Florida. The arrangement was made by Sara'o Bery of the distributor A24, the film's producers, and the college. Rivera was only ten years old at the time of the scholarship offer. His grades will be monitored in middle and high school so that he will be adequately prepared when the time comes for him to attend college. If Rivera eventually succeeds in attending and graduating from Rollins, Sean Baker believes that it may be the best thing to come out of his film.[53] For him, that would represent the film's true happy ending.

Conclusion

In his book *Indie 2.0*, Geoff King provides a broad overview of American indie cinema in the first decade of the twenty-first century. Since its resurgence in the 1980s and 1990s, American indie cinema has experienced a number of peaks and valleys. Its status continues to fluctuate as a result of industrial changes that continually threaten its position as an alternative practice. King discusses a number of discourses that surround indie cinema, including that it is in a permanent state of crisis, and he even suggests that "this is, in a sense, part of its definition."[1] King uses the word "indie" rather than "independent" to denote films that challenge conventional norms. He argues for "a strong vein of continuity in indie practice, both industrially and in the textual qualities through which individual features mark their distinctive attributes from those usually associated with the Hollywood mainstream."[2]

The rise of digital cinema and new distribution platforms has altered the landscape for indie filmmakers in the new century. Films can be made more cheaply than ever before, allowing filmmakers an opportunity to shoot features that can play at film festivals, in theaters, in independent showcases, and on streaming platforms. It is now possible to make low-budget films that gain a certain degree of critical recognition but end up having limited appeal within the broader marketplace. The work of Kelly Reichardt serves as a case in point. Although she has made seven highly acclaimed features, only three of her films—*Wendy and Lucy* (2008), *Meek's Cutoff* (2010), and *Certain Women* (2016)—have grossed more than $1 million at the box office. She explains, "Well, one thing is that the films have all been very small and I've really had complete freedom in making them. I have final cut, I don't have to adjust the script, and the people are either in or they're out. We take small amounts of money to make these films, in exchange for the artistic freedom I have."[3]

Indie filmmakers often have to make numerous compromises in order to obtain financing for larger-budget projects. In the new century, this has usually meant adding A-list stars to the production because it helps to sell the film at the box office. This in itself, however, often substantially changes the very nature of the film being made. Once he was able to obtain a substantially larger budget than ever before, Baker found himself under pressure to cast high-profile stars to play Halley. The names of pop celebrities such as Britney Spears, Miley Cyrus, and Ariana Grande were bandied about because they would raise the profile and market appeal of the movie.

Although Baker felt a responsibility to his financial backers, he was uncomfortable with such choices. He told an interviewer, "I mean, playing somebody who lives in poverty and you know they're one of the richest people would be a weird thing on many levels."[4] For Baker, casting a celebrity actor in that role would have been contrary to his aesthetic of social realism and undermined the credibility of his portrayal of a marginalized subculture of homeless families living in budget motels. Yet finding inexperienced and first-time actors, whether through street casting or social media, not only took an inordinate amount of time but represented a gamble.

Willem Dafoe ended up being the one well-known actor cast in a major role. He became an essential part of the film's success, especially after being nominated for an Academy Award.

Professional actors can rely on skills that developed over time, but first-time actors don't have that luxury, which places a heavier burden on the director to get them aligned with their characters. After the experience of working with Michelle Williams in *Wendy and Lucy*, Kelly Reichardt noted the difference between the two types of performers: "Working with really experienced actors who give you a variety of things, you have a lot to work with in the editing process. If you're working with a nonprofessional actor, you're more saying, 'I want you to be onscreen!' Then, that is what you have. You're not making a bunch of choices along the way."[5]

Many viewers might think that the actors in Reichardt's films are improvising, but that's not the case. Even though she has worked with a number of major actors at this point—Michelle Williams, Zoe Kazan, Paul Dano, Jesse Eisenberg, and Peter Sarsgaard—she wants them to adhere to the script. Reichardt explains, "It's weird, you know, if you open the doors to actors being able to bring their own ideas, it's a slippery slope, because it means that everyone wants to do it. Some people are better at it than other people. And mostly, I want people to stick to the script."[6]

Baker, on the other hand, is at heart an improviser. He is not afraid of negotiating that slippery slope when it comes to performers taking liberties with the script. It should be acknowledged that most films utilize some degree of improvisation, as there is usually some deviance from the script due to the vicissitudes of production. What Baker was attempting in *The Florida Project*, however, was quite unusual. Not many filmmakers would head into a major production with so many gaps in a script, or be willing to undertake such radical changes in the midst of shooting. In tracing the conception and evolution of the screen idea through its various stages of development, preproduction, and production, it becomes possible to understand the sheer complexity of the filmmaker's artistic method.

What stands out about *The Florida Project* are all the ways Baker refused to compromise his vision throughout the process. It becomes clear that in making the film on his own terms, Baker was performing a delicate high-wire act. The film had an extremely high degree of difficulty. The first risk involved casting inexperienced and first-time actors in so many of the roles, including four child actors that he found locally. Add to this the time constraints faced by the production due to the shortened number of hours the child actors could work and a shooting schedule of only thirty-five days, and Baker's achievement seems even more unlikely.

There were a number of logistical problems that would have made it an extremely difficult shoot by any standards. Baker wasn't filming on sets but in two of the budget motels, which he believed were an essential part of the authenticity of the film. Both motels were fully operational—they were open for business and had homeless families living in them. Although the two main locations were not the most hard-core budget motels along Route 192, the production nevertheless had to worry about such issues as security, unwanted intrusions, and the hazards of poverty. In addition, shooting a film in the heat of a Florida summer posed a major obstacle.

Baker's nimble approach is well suited to making low-budget films, but how would it fare on a production with a much larger budget? Luckily for Baker, he had sympathetic producers and financiers who seemed to grasp that the director's method of making films is unorthodox but essential to his success. Some members of the union crew were not prepared for a director who did not follow the type of protocols they expected on a professional set. Baker's impromptu decisions would rile any number of departments—from the script supervisor to hair and makeup, as well as costume and wardrobe. Baker became frustrated with the inflexibility of his crew, but they were equally frustrated with him. As Baker explains, "When you are working with a group of people that don't know your directing style and they're used to a very specific way of making films—a union crew, local crews—yeah, that was a problem."[7]

In *Rewriting Indie Cinema*, I trace the use of improvisation in indie cinema from its early roots at the beginning of the New American Cinema during the late 1950s and early 1960s.[8] At the time, the influential film critic Jonas Mekas valorized "spontaneity" as a rebellion against the staged and scripted aspect of Hollywood films, and saw improvisation as a means to revitalize American cinema. Looking at the history of indie cinema through this lens demonstrates that at various times, especially in the new century, the use of improvisation has helped indie filmmakers to create an alternative practice to mainstream cinema. Baker's struggles in making a larger-budget film prove instructive because of his refusal to compromise his artistic integrity despite the pressures he encountered during production. But what does this portend for his next film?

Critical and box office success generally leads to opportunities to work with an even larger budget. Following *Heaven*

Knows What, their gritty psychodrama about drug addicts surviving on the streets of Manhattan, Josh and Benny Safdie were able to make the crime thriller *Good Time* with a reported budget of $4.5 million.[9] This was mainly due to having cast Robert Pattinson in the lead role. The film grossed over $2 million domestically and nearly $3.3 million worldwide. The critical success of this film led to a greater breakthrough when the Safdies made their next film, *Uncut Gems*, for $19 million. The crime thriller, starring Adam Sandler, grossed $50 million domestically. *Good Time* and *Uncut Gems* are genre films, which gave them greater mass appeal.

Major streaming providers such as Amazon and Netflix recently have managed to create new financing opportunities for indie films. For instance, both were major buyers of independent films at the 2016 Sundance Film Festival. Due to their broader audiences, the digital distributors were more accepting of films with less traditional storylines. As Julia Greenberg explains in an article in *WIRED*, "The tech giants also have more leeway to experiment. Their subscription-based models mean they don't need every film to be a blockbuster. A single movie or show on Netflix and Amazon needn't appeal to everyone; the key for both platforms is making sure they offer enough of everything to attract anyone."[10]

In the four years since *The Florida Project* was released, the industry has undergone another major transformation. The biggest change has to do with the fact that funding has become much more difficult for smaller indie films to obtain as the major digital distributors have switched their priorities and focused on more high-profile films with A-list stars. One reason is the hope that such films will win Oscars for the streaming companies and give them greater prestige within the industry.[11] The worldwide COVID-19 pandemic has exacerbated the problem by shutting down not only festivals and movie theaters but productions as well. This has proven to be especially disastrous for indie filmmakers. Kelly Reichardt's latest film, *First Cow* (2020) played at the 2019 New York Film Festival but made only slightly over $100,000 in its brief theatrical run, which was cut short due to the health crisis. Indie filmmaker Robert Greene offers a sobering assessment of the current situation: "Before COVID, the US media landscape was already pushing us to devolve from being artists to being 'content creators.' This is what capitalism does: It flattens nuance, numbs our senses, and convinces us to sit back and accept the new normal."[12]

In retrospect, *The Florida Project* appears to represent a crossroads—not only for its director but for American indie cinema. For Baker's way of working and the kinds of socially concerned films that he is intent on producing, larger budgets are not necessarily cost effective. They also make it difficult for him to create intimate character studies rather than the plot-driven films favored by mass audiences. Like Kelly Reichardt, Baker also worries about losing artistic control. He explains, "I don't think at this point I could ever jump above a certain budget level and retain final cut, which is very important to me. If one change was made in the movie that was out of my control, it would be very difficult for me to ever accept that as my own."[13] The struggle between art and commerce is an age-old dilemma. Yet it is one that has become an even greater challenge for dedicated indie filmmakers like Sean Baker at the start of the third decade of the twenty-first century.

Acknowledgments

This book grew out of a paper I gave on the films of Sean Baker at the 2018 Society for Cinema and Media Studies (SCMS) Conference in Toronto. In January 2019, Donna Kornhaber, one of the co-organizers of the panel, contacted me about a new series she was editing for the University of Texas Press called 21st Century Film Essentials, which would focus on individual films. I could write on any independent film I chose, but she specifically asked if I would consider writing about Sean Baker's *The Florida Project*. For me, it represented a different kind of project, especially because the books in the series were being targeted to a general audience. Although I have always tried to write more broadly than to a strictly academic audience, I considered writing such a book to be a challenge. In effect, I put aside two other potential projects to concentrate on this one.

I was an early supporter of Sean Baker's work following the releases of *Take Out* and *Prince of Broadway* in 2008. I had interviewed him at some length about *Tangerine* (2017) for my last book, *Rewriting Indie Cinema* (2019), and I decided that *The Florida Project* would be an excellent subject. When I contacted Sean, he expressed immediate enthusiasm. I cautioned him that the book would involve a great deal of work on his part. I also explained that I could only write a book if granted complete access to materials and personnel connected with the project. Sean needed to consult with associates, but he wound up giving a thumbs-up to the project and promised to assist in any way possible.

Frankly, this book could not have been written without the generous cooperation of Baker and his trusted team of collaborators. I have to say that, despite how busy everyone's schedule was, they always made it a priority to talk with me and answer my myriad questions. My heartfelt gratitude goes to Sean Baker, Samantha Quan, Chris Bergoch, Kevin Chinoy, Shih-Ching Tsou, Stephonik Youth, Alexis Zabé, Jennifer Conrader, Patti Wiley, and Alex Coco. Sammy Quan deserves a special shout-out for always responding promptly to my queries, and Alex Coco, who took a particular interest in the book, never failed to provide information that I needed in a timely manner. Thanks to Marc Schmidt and A24 for allowing me to use their photos.

Thanks to Donna Kornhaber for recruiting me for the series, being an engaged series editor, and providing five pages of detailed notes on the manuscript. I am grateful to the outside readers for their valuable feedback, especially Claire Perkins, who self-identified, for her enthusiastic response. I very much appreciated working with Jim Burr, who has been as superb a senior editor as any author could want. Thanks to the assistant editor Sarah McGavick for her help, especially regarding permissions; to Sarah Hudgens for her expert copyediting; and to Lynne Ferguson for overseeing the book during production.

Like filmmaking, writing a book is a collaborative endeavor. Mike King and Nancy Mladenoff read early versions of the manuscript and made insightful suggestions. My former colleagues Kelley Conway and David Bordwell both made significant contributions and provided sound advice whenever called upon. Kait Fyfe did a great job of pulling frame grabs from the film and making sure they were of high quality. Nancy Mladenoff has always been a loyal booster of my book projects, even when it takes time away from other aspects of our lives.

I first met David Bordwell in grad school fifty years ago, and we later became colleagues at the University of Wisconsin–Madison. When I began to write books on film after a career as a filmmaker, he was the person who took my writing most seriously. David's own books have been an incredible source of knowledge and inspiration. This book is dedicated to him.

Notes

INTRODUCTION

1. Unless otherwise indicated, all box office figures are taken from Box Office Mojo: boxofficemojo.com.
2. Sean Baker quoted in Danny Leigh, "The Florida Project's Sean Baker: 'I Wanted the Kids to Be the Kings and Queens of Their Domain,'" *The Guardian*, November 2, 2017, https://www.theguardian.com/film/2017/nov/02/sean -baker-florida-project-kids-kings-and-queens-their-domain.
3. Ken Loach quoted in Graham Fuller, ed., *Loach on Loach* (London: Faber and Faber, 1998), 114.
4. Gilles Mouëllic, *Improvising Cinema* (Amsterdam: Amsterdam University Press, 2013), 11.
5. Mouëllic, *Improvising Cinema*, 165.
6. Ken Loach quoted in Fuller, *Loach on Loach*, 114.
7. Samantha Lay, *British Social Realism: From Documentary to Brit Grit* (London: Wallflower, 2002), 6.
8. Julia Hallam and Margaret Marshment, *Realism and Popular Cinema* (Manchester: Manchester University Press, 2000), 184. I am aware that David Forrest and other scholars have been critical of the concept of social realism. For a brief summary of such critiques, see Jennifer Kirby, "American Utopia: Socio-economic Critique and Utopia in *American Honey* and *The Florida Project*," *Senses of Cinema*, October 2019, http://sensesofcinema.com/2019/feature-articles /american-utopia-socio-economic-critique-and-utopia-in -american-honey-and-the-florida-project/.

9. Glorianna Davenport, "When Place Becomes Character: A Critical Framing of Place for Mobile and Situated Narratives," MIT Media Lab, https://mf.media.mit.edu /pubs/other/CharacterPlace.pdf.

10. Davenport, "When Place Becomes Character."

11. Sean Baker quoted in Amy Taubin, "Interview: Sean Baker," *Film Comment*, September 4, 2017, https://www.filmcomment .com/blog/interview-sean-baker-florida-project/.

12. Sean Baker quoted in Rod Bastanmehr, "'Tangerine' Was Shot on an iPhone, but Director Sean Baker Still Pines for Celluloid," *Vice*, July 11, 2015, https://www.vice.com/en_us/article /exqzak/talking-tangerine-with-filmmaker-sean-baker-253.

13. Sean Baker quoted in KC Ifeanyi, "Why Sean Baker's 'The Florida Project' Put Him at a Creative Crossroads," *Fast Company*, October 19, 2017, https://www.fastcompany .com/40481962/why-sean-bakers-the-florida-project-put -him-at-a-creative-crossroads.

ORIGINS OF THE FILM

1. Sean Baker, Skype interview with author, June 27, 2019.

2. See Leigh, "The Florida Project's Sean Baker."

3. Sean Baker, Skype interview with author, June 27, 2019.

4. Sean Baker quoted in Leigh, "The Florida Project's Sean Baker."

5. For a discussion of different forms of improvisation— the spontaneous, the planned, and the rehearsed—see J. J. Murphy, *Rewriting Indie Cinema: Improvisation, Psychodrama, and the Screenplay* (New York: Columbia University Press, 2019), 10–13.

6. "Bonus Features: The Making of *Four Letter Words*," *Four Letter Words*, directed by Sean Baker (Los Angeles, CA: Vanguard Quality Independent Cinema, 2002), DVD.

7. Sean Baker quoted in "Bonus Features: The Making of *Four Letter Words*."

8. Sean Baker, Skype interview with author, June 27, 2019. For a detailed discussion of mumblecore, see Geoff King, *Indie*

2.0: Change and Continuity in Contemporary Indie Film
(New York: Columbia University Press, 2014), 122–168.

9. Sean Baker, Skype interview with author, June 27, 2019.

10. Sean Baker, voice text message to author, December 22, 2019.

11. See Ryan Koo, "'Prince of Broadway' Director Sean Baker on No-Budget Filmmaking, Improvisation, and Long Release Cycles," No Film School, October 18, 2011, https://nofilmschool.com/2011/10/sean-baker-prince-of-broadway-interview.

12. See Koo, "'Prince of Broadway' Director Sean Baker."

13. Sean Baker quoted in Anna Husted, "Interview: Sean Baker, 'Starlet,'" FilmLinc Daily, November 9, 2012, https://www.filmlinc.org/daily/qa-with-director-sean-baker-starlet/.

14. Peter Broderick, "How to Be Unstoppable: Sean Baker and the Digital Filmmaking Revolution," *IndieWire*, July 10, 2015, https://www.indiewire.com/2015/07/how-to-be-unstoppable-sean-baker-and-the-digital-filmmaking-revolution-247890/.

15. Ian W. Macdonald, *Screenwriting Poetics and the Screen Idea* (New York: Palgrave Macmillan, 2013), 4–5.

16. Macdonald, *Screenwriting Poetics*, 6–7.

17. Macdonald, *Screenwriting Poetics*, 11.

18. Macdonald, *Screenwriting Poetics*, 73–74.

19. *60 Minutes*, "Hard Times Generation: Homeless Kids," produced by Robert G. Anderson, Nicole Young, and Daniel Ruetenik, aired March 6, 2011, on CBS, https://www.youtube.com/watch?v=dK_RnxYdrqU.

20. Saki Knafo, "Homeless Children Living on the Highway to Disney World," *HuffPost*, last updated April 22, 2012, https://www.huffpost.com/entry/homeless-children-disney-world_n_1420702.

21. Knafo, "Homeless Children Living on the Highway."

22. Knafo, "Homeless Children Living on the Highway."

23. Chris Bergoch, email correspondence with Sean Baker, April 20, 2012.

24. Chris Bergoch, email correspondence with Sean Baker, April 20, 2012.

25. Chris Bergoch, email correspondence with Sean Baker, April 20, 2012.

26. Sean Baker, email correspondence with Chris Bergoch, April 20, 2012.

27. Chris Bergoch, email correspondence with Sean Baker, April 21, 2019.

28. Chris Bergoch, email correspondence with Sean Baker, April 21, 2012.

29. Chris Bergoch, email correspondence with Sean Baker, April 23, 2012.

30. Sean Baker, email correspondence with Chris Bergoch, May 4, 2012.

31. Sean Baker and Chris Bergoch, "Scriptment: *The Florida Project*" (unpublished, May 27, 2012).

32. Barbara DeLollis, "Homeless Man Arrested in Disney-Area Hotel Scam," *Detroit Free Press*, July 1, 2012.

33. Monivette Cordeiro, "'The Florida Project' Portrays the Underbelly of Kissimmee's Famous Tourist Trap," *Orlando Weekly*, October 4, 2017, https://www.orlandoweekly.com /orlando/the-florida-project-portrays-the-underbelly-of -kissimmees-famous-tourist-strip-we-talk-to-some-of-the -real-people-living-the-low-rent-mote/Content?oid =7400628&showFullText=true.

34. Cordeiro, "'The Florida Project' Portrays the Underbelly."

35. Anika Myers Palm, "Meth Lab Causes Explosion at Kissimmee Motel," *Orlando Sentinel*, January 22, 2010, https://www.orlandosentinel.com/news/os-xpm -2010-01-22-os-osceola-meth-lab-20100122-story.html.

36. Taubin, "Interview: Sean Baker."

37. Sean Baker and Chris Bergoch, "Director's Statement, International Pitch: *The Florida Project*," April 2016, 1.

38. Baker and Bergoch, "Director's Statement," 1.

39. In various versions of the screenplay, the character name is spelled "Haley," but the spelling changed to "Halley" for the

actual film. For clarity and consistency, I have used "Halley" throughout.

40. Sean Baker and Chris Bergoch, "Screenplay: *The Florida Project*" (unpublished, April 20, 2016), 41.

41. Baker and Bergoch, "Screenplay: *The Florida Project*," 51.

42. Baker and Bergoch, "Screenplay: *The Florida Project*," 51–52.

43. Shih-Ching Tsou, interview with author, November 25, 2019.

44. Shih-Ching Tsou, interview with author, November 25, 2019.

45. Sean Baker and Chris Bergoch, "Shooting Script: *The Florida Project* (White Production Draft)" (unpublished, June 27, 2016), 97.

46. See Kathryn Millard, *Screenwriting in a Digital Era* (New York: Palgrave Macmillan, 2014), 35.

47. Vera John-Steiner, *Creative Collaboration* (Oxford, UK: Oxford University Press, 2006), 76.

48. John-Steiner, *Creative Collaboration*, 70.

49. Chris Bergoch, Skype interview with author, June 24, 2019.

50. Taubin, "Interview: Sean Baker."

51. Sean Baker quoted in Taubin, "Interview: Sean Baker."

52. Sean Baker quoted in Taubin, "Interview: Sean Baker."

53. See Syd Field, *Screenplay: The Foundations of Screenwriting* (New York: Dell Publishing, 1982).

54. Sean Baker quoted in "BAFTA Screenwriters' Lecture Series: Sean Baker," BAFTA, November 22, 2017, http://www.bafta.org/media-centre/transcripts/bafta-screenwriters-lecture-series-sean-baker.

55. Sean Baker quoted in "BAFTA Screenwriters Lecture Series."

56. Chris Bergoch, Skype interview with author, June 24, 2019.

57. Chris Bergoch, Skype interview with author, June 24, 2019.

58. Chris Bergoch, Skype interview with author, June 24, 2019.

59. Chris Bergoch, Skype interview with author, June 24, 2019.

60. Chris Bergoch, Skype interview with author, June 24, 2019.

61. Chris Bergoch, Skype interview with author, June 24, 2019.

62. Baker's Chihuahuas, Bunsen and Boonee (who played Starlet) at one point were going to appear in the film (and

are still listed in the final script), and a bulldog was also
considered before practicality set in.

63. Sean Baker, Skype interview with author, June 29, 2019.
64. Sean Baker, Skype interview with author, June 29, 2019.
65. Sean Baker, Skype interview with author, June 29, 2019.
66. Sean Baker, Skype interview with author, June 29, 2019.
67. Sean Baker, Skype interview with author, June 29, 2019.
68. Sean Baker quoted in "Bonus Features: *Under the Rainbow*,
    directed by Alex Coco," *The Florida Project*, directed by Sean
    Baker (Los Angeles, CA: Lionsgate, 2017), Blu-ray.
69. Ken Loach quoted in Fuller, *Loach on Loach*, 18.
70. Sean Baker, Skype interview with author, June 29, 2019.
71. See Murphy, *Rewriting Indie Cinema*.
72. Chris Bergoch quoted in Kee Chang, "Q&A with
    Chris Bergoch," *Anthem*, October 15, 2017, http://
    anthemmagazine.com/qa-with-chris-bergoch/.
73. Chris Bergoch quoted in Chang, "Q&A with Chris Bergoch."
74. Kevin Chinoy, email to author, January 2, 2020.
75. Kevin Chinoy, email to author, January 2, 2020.
76. Kevin Chinoy, email to author, January 2, 2020.
77. Kevin Chinoy, Skype interview with author, November 18,
    2019.
78. Stephonik Youth quoted in Matt Grobar, " 'The Florida
    Project' Production Designer on Tracking Down Dreary
    Pastel-Colored Locations for Dark Fairy Tale," *Deadline*,
    January 1, 2018, https://deadline.com/2018/01/the-florida
    -project-stephonik-youth-production-design-interview
    -news-1202230046/.
79. Chris Bergoch quoted in Chang, "Q&A with Chris Bergoch."
80. Sean Baker quoted in Sean Baker, "I am Sean Baker, director
    of Tangerine–Ask Me Anything!" Reddit, March 8, 2016,
    https://www.reddit.com/r/TrueFilm/comments/49jy9b
    /i_am_sean_baker_director_of_tangerine_ask_me/.
81. Lay, *British Social Realism*, 34.
82. Kevin Chinoy, Skype interview with author, November 18,
    2019.

83. Kevin Chinoy, email to author, January 2, 2020.

84. Patti Wiley, Skype interview with author, December 21, 2019.

85. Patti Wiley, Skype interview with author, December 21, 2019.

86. Patti Wiley, Skype interview with author, December 21, 2019.

87. Samantha Quan, Skype interview with author, June 17, 2019.

88. Kevin Chinoy, Skype interview with author, November 18, 2019.

89. Samantha Quan, Skype interview with author, June 17, 2019.

90. Samantha Quan, Skype interview with author, June 17, 2019.

91. Samantha Quan, Skype interview with author, June 17, 2019.

92. Samantha Quan, Skype interview with author, June 17, 2019.

93. Samantha Quan, Skype interview with author, June 17, 2019.

94. Samantha Quan, Skype interview with author, June 17, 2019.

95. Samantha Quan, Skype interview with author, June 17, 2019.

96. Samantha Quan, Skype interview with author, June 17, 2019.

97. Samantha Quan, Skype interview with author, June 17, 2019.

98. Sean Baker, Skype interview with author, July 1, 2019.

99. Sean Baker quoted in Taubin, "Interview: Sean Baker."

100. Samantha Quan, Skype interview with author, June 17, 2019.

101. Willem Dafoe quoted in "Bonus Features," *The Florida Project*, directed by Sean Baker (Los Angeles, CA: Lionsgate, 2017), Blu-ray.

102. Sean Baker quoted in Nick Allen, "When You Wish upon a Star: Sean Baker on the 'The Florida Project,'" Roger Ebert, October 3, 2017, https://www.rogerebert.com/interviews /when-you-wish-upon-a-star-sean-baker-on-the-florida -project.

THE MAKING OF *THE FLORIDA PROJECT*

1. Sean Baker, Skype interview with author, December 22, 2019.

2. Sean Baker, Skype interview with author, December 22, 2019.

3. Alexis Zabé, Skype interview with author, December 23, 2019.

4. Alexis Zabé, Skype interview with author, December 23, 2019.

5. Alexis Zabé, Skype interview with author, December 23, 2019.

6. Alexis Zabé quoted in Matt Grobar, "'The Florida Project' Cinematographer Alexis Zabe on Gorgeously-Realized 'Little

Rascals' for the 21st Century," *Deadline*, December 18, 2017, https://deadline.com/2017/12/the-florida-project-alexis-zabe-cinematography-interview-news-1202224249/.

7. Alexis Zabé quoted in Grobar, " 'The Florida Project' Cinematographer."

8. Alexis Zabé, Skype interview with author, December 23, 2019.

9. Alexis Zabé quoted in Grobar, " 'The Florida Project' Cinematographer."

10. Alexis Zabé quoted in Grobar, " 'The Florida Project' Cinematographer."

11. Stephonik Youth, Skype interview with author, December 8, 2019.

12. "Bonus Features: *Under the Rainbow.*"

13. Kevin Chinoy, Skype interview with author, November 18, 2019.

14. Kevin Chinoy, Skype interview with author, November 18, 2019.

15. Alexis Zabé, Skype interview with author, December 23, 2019.

16. Alexis Zabé, Skype interview with author, December 23, 2019.

17. Sean Baker, "Cuts, Both Ways: Sean Baker's 11 Rules for Editing Your Own Films," *MovieMaker*, October 3, 2017, https://www.moviemaker.com/sean-baker-11-rules-for-editing-your-own-films/.

18. Alex Coco, Skype interview with author, November 20, 2019.

19. Kevin Chinoy, Skype interview with author, November 18, 2019.

20. Kevin Chinoy, Skype interview with author, November 18, 2019.

21. Mouëllic, *Improvising Cinema*, 11.

22. Alexis Zabé, Skype interview with author, December 23, 2019.

23. Alex Coco, Skype interview with author, November 20, 2019.

24. Alex Coco, Skype interview with author, November 20, 2019.

25. Kevin Chinoy quoted in Louise Tutt, "Sean Baker on the Story behind 'The Florida Project,' " *Screen Daily*, December 22, 2017, https://www.screendaily.com/interviews/sean-baker-on-the-story-behind-the-florida-project-/5125160.article.

26. Stephonik Youth, interview with author, December 8, 2019.

27. Stephonik Youth, interview with author, December 8, 2019.
28. Sean Baker quoted in "Bonus Features: *Under the Rainbow*."
29. Alexis Zabé, Skype interview with author, December 23, 2019.
30. Alex Coco, Skype interview with author, November 20, 2019.
31. Alex Coco, Skype interview with author, November 20, 2019.
32. Sean Baker quoted in "Bonus Features: *Under the Rainbow*."
33. Alexis Zabé, Skype interview with author, December 23, 2019.
34. Alexis Zabé, Skype interview with author, December 23, 2019.
35. Alexis Zabé, Skype interview with author, December 23, 2019.
36. Sean Baker quoted in Chris O'Falt, "'The Florida Project': Sean Baker Almost Lost His Crew and Movie during Production," *IndieWire*, October 6, 2017, https://www.indiewire.com/2017/10/florida-project-sean-baker-almost-lost-crew-avoids-disaster-1201884419/.
37. Sean Baker quoted in O'Falt, "'The Florida Project.'"
38. Alexis Zabé, Skype interview with author, December 23, 2019.
39. Alexis Zabé, Skype interview with author, December 23, 2019.
40. Alexis Zabé, Skype interview with author, December 23, 2019.
41. Alexis Zabé, Skype interview with author, December 23, 2019.
42. Alex Coco, Skype interview with author, November 20, 2019.
43. Sean Baker quoted in O'Falt, "'The Florida Project.'"
44. See Chris O'Falt, "Sean Baker Cut Up Paul Thomas Anderson Long Takes to See If a Doc-Style Steadicam Would Work on 'The Florida Project,'" *IndieWire*, November 16, 2017, https://www.indiewire.com/2017/11/florida-project-director-sean-baker-steadicam-paul-thomas-anderson-filmmaker-toolkit-podcast-episode-41-1201898335/.
45. Sean Baker quoted in Allen, "When You Wish upon a Star."
46. Sean Baker quoted in Allen, "When You Wish upon a Star."
47. Sean Baker, Skype interview with author, June 27, 2019.
48. Call sheet, *The Florida Project* (unpublished, August 17, 2016). Provided by Alex Coco as an attachment in email to author, November 25, 2019.
49. Sean Baker quoted in O'Falt, "'The Florida Project.'"
50. Sean Baker, Skype interview with author, June 27, 2019.
51. Sean Baker, Skype interview with author, June 27, 2019.
52. Sean Baker, Skype interview with author, July 1, 2019.

53. Sean Baker quoted in Taubin, "Interview: Sean Baker."

54. Kevin Chinoy, Skype interview with author, November 18, 2018.

55. Cher Krause Knight, *Power and Paradise in Walt Disney's World* (Gainesville: University Press of Florida, 2014), 16.

56. See Knight, *Power and Paradise in Walt Disney's World*, 18.

57. Knight, *Power and Paradise in Walt Disney's World*, 18.

58. Sean Baker quoted in Brian Formo, "Sean Baker on 'The Florida Project' and His Camaraderie with the Safdie Brothers," *Collider*, October 13, 2017, https://collider.com /sean-baker-the-florida-project-interview/#amateur-cast.

59. Baker, "Cuts, Both Ways."

60. Sean Baker, Skype interview with author, July 1, 2019.

61. Alex Coco, Skype interview with author, November 20, 2019.

62. Alexis Zabé, Skype interview with author, December 23, 2019.

63. Alexis Zabé, Skype interview with author, December 23, 2019.

64. Sean Baker quoted in Alexander Hakimi, "'The Florida Project' Director Sean Baker on Working with Untrained Actors and Secret Filming in Disney World," *Paper*, October 20, 2017, http://www.papermag.com/the-florida-project -director-sean-baker-on-working-with-untrained-actos-and -secret-filming-in-disney-world-2499057069.html.

65. Kevin Chinoy, Skype interview with author, November 18, 2019.

66. See Anita Busch and Patty Leon, "'Midnight Rider' Director Randall Miller Freed from Jail in Shock Ruling—Update," *Deadline*, March 23, 2016, https://deadline.com/2016/03 /midnight-rider-director-randall-miller-released-jail-sarah -jones-1201724651/. Part of the sentencing stipulated that Miller was, in effect, "prohibited from serving as director, first assistant director or supervisor with responsibility for safety in any film production" for a period of ten years. In 2019, Miller directed a film, *Higher Grounds*, in Europe. Miller received a strong reprimand from the judge, but no additional jail time.

67. Sean Baker, Skype interview with author, December 22, 2019.

68. Chris Bergoch, Skype interview with author, June 24, 2019.

69. Sean Baker quoted in "BAFTA Screenwriters Lecture Series."

70. Sean Baker quoted in "BAFTA Screenwriters Lecture Series."

71. Sean Baker, Skype interview with author, December 22, 2019.

72. Sean Baker, Skype interview with author, December 22, 2019.

73. Sean Baker, Skype Interview with author, December 22, 2019.

74. Sean Baker, Skype interview with author, December 22, 2019.

75. J. Brandon Colvin, "The Other Side of Frontality: Dorsality in European Art Cinema," *New Review of Film and Television Studies* 15, no. 2 (2017): 194.

76. Baker has expressed regret that the British tourist who buys the MagicBands looks too much like Macon Blair, who plays the john, which has caused some confusion in viewers. Sean Baker, Skype interview with author, December 22, 2019.

77. Alexis Zabé, Skype interview with author, December 23, 2019.

78. Alexis Zabé, Skype interview with author, December 23, 2019.

79. Sean Baker and Chris Bergoch, "Final Production Draft: *The Florida Project*" (unpublished, July 31, 2016), 83.

80. Samantha Quan, Skype interview with author, June 17, 2019.

81. Baker, "Cuts, Both Ways."

82. Baker and Bergoch, "Final Production Draft."

83. This represents an example of the film's use of creative geography in the fictional story world. In actuality, the distance between the Paradise Inn and the Magic Kingdom is over ten miles.

RECEPTION

1. Baker and Bergoch, "Final Production Draft."

2. Chris Bergoch, Skype interview with author, June 24, 2019.

3. Sean Baker quoted in Allen, "When You Wish upon a Star."

4. Matt Zoller Seitz, "*Escape from Tomorrow* (2013)," Roger Ebert, October 11, 2013, https://www.rogerebert.com /reviews/escape-from-tomorrow-2013.

5. Matt Zoller Seitz, "*Escape from Tomorrow* (2013)."

6. See Katie Kilkenny, "Abigail Disney Calls for 'Dignity' and 'Human Rights' for Disneyland Employees," *Hollywood*

Reporter, July 17, 2019, https://www.hollywoodreporter.com /news/abigail-disney-calls-dignity-disneyland-employees -1224936.

7. Abigail Disney quoted in Kilkenny, "Abigail Disney Calls for 'Dignity.'"

8. Kevin Chinoy, email to author, January 3, 2020.

9. Kelefa Sanneh, "Outside Shot: The Safdie Brothers' New Film Is a Dizzying Ode to New York—and Maybe a Hit," *New Yorker*, December 16, 2019, 36.

10. Alexis Zabé, Skype interview with author, December 23, 2019.

11. Alex Coco, Skype interview with author, November 20, 2019.

12. Alex Coco, email to author, January 4, 2020.

13. Information provided by Alex Coco in email to author, January 4, 2020.

14. Samantha Quan, email to author, November 13, 2019.

15. Kevin Chinoy, Skype interview with author, November 18, 2019.

16. Sean Baker quoted in Taubin, "Interview: Sean Baker."

17. Chris Bergoch quoted in Monivette Cordeiro, "'The Florida Project' Stars Talk Ice Cream, Orange Bird and Bittersweet Endings," *Orlando Weekly*, October 17, 2017, https://www .orlandoweekly.com/Blogs/archives/2017/10/17/the-florida -project-stars-talk-ice-cream-orange-bird-and-bittersweet -endings.

18. Sean Baker quoted in Cordeiro, "'The Florida Project' Stars Talk Ice Cream."

19. Michael Koretsky, "The Florida Project: Keep on Running," *Reverse Shot*, October 2, 2017, http://www.reverseshot.org /reviews/entry/2360/florida_project.

20. David Rooney, "'The Florida Project': Film Review / Cannes 2017," *Hollywood Reporter*, May 23, 2017, https://www.hollywoodreporter.com/review/florida-project -cannes-2017-1006653.

21. Corey Atad, "*The Florida Project* Has the Most Perfect Ending of Any Movie in Years," *Slate*, October 19, 2017,

https://slate.com/culture/2017/10/the-florida-project
-s-ending-is-perfect.html.

22. Anne Helen Petersen, "The Director of the Year's Most-
Hyped Movie Isn't Playing Hollywood's Game," *BuzzFeed
News*, November 19, 2017, https://www.buzzfeednews
.com/article/annehelenpetersen/sean-baker-isnt-playing
-hollywoods-game.

23. Robert Koehler quoted in Richard Porton, "Life on the
Margins: An Interview with Sean Baker," *Cineaste*, Winter
2017, 22.

24. Sean Baker quoted in Porton, "Life on the Margins," 25.

25. Sean Baker quoted in Formo, "Sean Baker on 'The Florida
Project.'"

26. Erving Goffman, *Stigma: Notes on the Management of
Spoiled Identity* (New York: Touchstone, 1963), 5.

27. Rev. Mary Lee Downey quoted in Lilla Ross, "'Florida
Project' Film Assisted by Florida Clergy," Florida Conference
of the United Methodist Church, December 5, 2017,
https://www.flumc.org/newsdetail/rev-mary-downey-major
-player-for-independent-film-homeless-10072280.

28. Sean Baker quoted in Porton, "Life on the Margins," 25.

29. Rooney, "'The Florida Project': Film Review / Cannes 2017."

30. Owen Gleiberman, "Why Bria Vinaite, as a Loving Mother
from Hell, Is the 'The Florida Project's' Not-So-Secret
Weapon," *Variety*, October 22, 2017, https://variety.com
/2017/film/columns/the-florida-project-bria-vinaite
-1202595987/.

31. Gleiberman, "Why Bria Vinaite."

32. Anne Thompson, "Why Sean Baker's 'The Florida Project'
Was the Hot Buy of Cannes," *IndieWire*, May 30, 2017,
https://www.indiewire.com/2017/05/the-florida-project
-a24-sean-baker-willem-dafoe-cannes-2017-1201833665/.

33. Olivia Ovenden, "The Oscar's Snub of 'The Florida Project'
Shows Hollywood Hasn't Really Changed," *Esquire*, January
24, 2018, https://www.esquire.com/uk/culture/film
/a15853873/the-florida-project-oscar-snub/.

34. Ovenden, "Oscar's Snub of 'The Florida Project.'"

35. Ovenden, "Oscar's Snub of 'The Florida Project.'"

36. Ovenden, "Oscar's Snub of 'The Florida Project.'"

37. Willem Dafoe quoted in Nick Romano, "Willem Dafoe Is Thrilled to Bring Oscar-Level Awareness to *The Florida Project*," *Entertainment Weekly*, January 23, 2018, https://ew.com/oscars/2018/01/23/oscars-2018-willem-dafoe-the-florida-project/.

38. Mary Kaye Schilling, "'The Florida Project' Was Robbed by the Oscars, Despite Being One of 2018's Most Powerful Movies," *Newsweek*, January 23, 2018, https://www.newsweek.com/florida-project-oscar-sub-sean-baker-brooklynn-prince-willem-dafoe-788156#slideshow/788335.

39. Schilling, "'The Florida Project' Was Robbed."

40. Scott Russell, "*The Florida Project* Deserved a Best Picture Nomination," *Paste*, March 3, 2018, https://www.pastemagazine.com/articles/2018/03/the-florida-project-deserved-a-best-picture-nomina.html.

41. Russell, "*The Florida Project* Deserved."

42. Sean Fitz-Gerald, "What It's Like to Be Snubbed by the Oscars," *Thrillist*, March 2, 2018, https://www.thrillist.com/entertainment/nation/oscar-snub-2018-the-florida-project-sean-baker-interview.

43. Shih-Ching Tsou, interview with author, November 25, 2019.

44. Shih-Ching Tsou, interview with author, November 25, 2019.

45. Justin Chang, "Review: Sean Baker's 'The Florida Project' Is a Magnificent Portrait of a Joyous, Troubled Childhood," *Los Angeles Times*, October 5, 2017, https://www.latimes.com/entertainment/movies/la-et-mn-the-florida-project-review-20171005-story.html.

46. Petersen, "Director of the Year's Most-Hyped Movie."

47. A. O. Scott, "Best Movies of 2017," *New York Times*, December 6, 2017, https://www.nytimes.com/2017/12/06/movies/best-movies.html.

48. Bria Vinaite quoted in Adam White, "The Florida Project's Bria Vinaite: 'People Assume I'm This Trashy Motel Girl, but I Know I Can Do More,'" *Independent*, July 31, 2019,

https://www.independent.co.uk/arts-entertainment/films
/features/bria-vinaite-interview-florida-project-balance-not
-symmetry-biffy-clyro-a9027441.html.
49. Sanneh, "Outside Shot," 35.
50. Josh Safdie quoted in Sanneh, "Outside Shot," 35.
51. Sean Baker quoted in Jenna Marotta, "'The Florida Project':
How Sean Baker and His Collaborators Used Instagram,
Target, and Motels to Find Its Cast," *IndieWire*, December
15, 2017, https://www.indiewire.com/2017/12/the-florida
-project-sean-baker-casting-instagram-1201907884/.
52. Jennifer Conrader, Skype interview with author, December 21,
2019.
53. Sean Baker, Skype interview with author, July 1, 2019.

CONCLUSION

1. King, *Indie 2.0*, 10.
2. King, *Indie 2.0*, 2.
3. Kelly Reichardt quoted in Katherine Fusco and Nicole
Seymour, *Kelly Reichardt* (Urbana: University of Illinois
Press, 2017), 113.
4. Sean Baker quoted in Tatiana Siegel, "How 'The Florida
Project' Cast Its Breakout Kid Stars in Target and a Motel,"
Hollywood Reporter, November 17, 2017, https://www
.hollywoodreporter.com/features/how-florida-project-cast
-breakout-kid-stars-target-a-motel-1057876.
5. Kelly Reichardt quoted in Fusco and Seymour, *Kelly
Reichardt*, 118.
6. Kelly Reichardt quoted in Fusco and Seymour, *Kelly
Reichardt*, 119.
7. Sean Baker quoted in O'Falt, "'The Florida Project.'"
8. See Murphy, *Rewriting Indie Cinema*.
9. Sanneh, "Outside Shot," 34.
10. Julia Greenberg, "Netflix and Amazon Offer Indie
Filmmakers Hope (And Lots of Money)," *WIRED*, January
28, 2016, https://www.wired.com/2016/01/netflix-and
-amazon-offer-indie-filmmakers-hope-and-lots-of
-money/.

11. See Kevin Tran, "Why the Film Festival Circuit Is So Important for Video Streamers," *Variety*, October 6, 2020, https://variety.com/vip/why-the-film-festival-circuit-is-so-important-for-video-streamers-1234793148/.

12. Robert Greene and Cecilia Aldarondo, "Where Does Independent Documentary Go from Here?," *Hyperallergic*, September 21, 2020, https://hyperallergic.com/588097/state-of-documentary-covid-filmmaker-conversation/?mc_cid=415903c4f4&mc_eid=2ba111f277.

13. Sean Baker quoted in Kyle Buchanan, "'I Only Have My Chihuahuas': Why *The Florida Project*'s Sean Baker Won't Sell Out," *Vulture*, November 2017, https://www.vulture.com/2017/11/the-florida-project-director-sean-baker-explains-his-process.html.

Bibliography

Baron, Cynthia, and Sharon Marie Carnicke. *Reframing Screen Performance*. Ann Arbor: University of Michigan Press, 2008.

Baron, Cynthia, Diane Carson, and Frank P. Tomasulo, eds. *More Than a Method: Trends and Traditions in Contemporary Film Performance*. Detroit, MI: Wayne State University Press, 2004.

Belgrad, Daniel. *The Culture of Spontaneity: Improvisation and the Arts in Postwar America*. Chicago: The University of Chicago Press, 1998.

Bordwell, David. *The Way Hollywood Tells It: Story and Style in Modern Movies*. Berkeley: University of California Press, 2006.

Cornic, Stefan, ed. *Morris Engel and Ruth Orkin: Outside—From Street Photography to Filmmaking*. Translated by William Snow. Paris: Carlotta Films, 2014.

Field, Syd. *Screenplay: The Foundations of Screenwriting*. New York: Dell Publishing, 1982.

Forrest, David. *Social Realism, Art, Nationhood, and Politics*. Newcastle upon Tyne, UK: Cambridge Scholars Publishing, 2013.

Frost, Anthony, and Ralph Yarrow. *Improvisation in Drama, Theatre and Performance: History, Practice, Theory*. 3rd ed. London: Palgrave, 2016.

Fuller, Graham, ed. *Loach on Loach*. London: Faber and Faber, 1998.

Fusco, Katherine, and Nicole Seymour. *Kelly Reichardt*. Urbana: University of Illinois Press, 2017.

Glick, Joshua. *Los Angeles Documentary and the Production of Public History, 1958–1977*. Oakland: University of California Press, 2018.

Goffman, Erving. *The Presentation of Self in Everyday Life*. New York: Anchor Books, 1959.

Goffman, Erving. *Stigma: Notes on the Management of Spoiled Identity*. New York: Touchstone, 1963.

Hallam, Julia, and Margaret Marshment. *Realism and Popular Cinema*. Manchester: Manchester University Press, 2000.

John-Steiner, Vera. *Creative Collaboration*. Oxford, UK: Oxford University Press, 2000.

King, Geoff. *American Independent Cinema*. Bloomington: Indiana University Press, 2005.

King, Geoff, ed. *A Companion to American Indie Film*. Malden, MA: Wiley Blackwell, 2017.

King, Geoff. *Indie 2.0: Change and Continuity in Contemporary American Indie Film*. New York: Columbia University Press, 2014.

Knight, Cher Krause. *Power and Paradise in Walt Disney's World*. Gainesville: University Press of Florida, 2014.

Lay, Samantha. *British Social Realism: From Documentary to Brit Grit*. London: Wallflower, 2002.

Lipman, Ross. "Kent Mackenzie's *The Exiles*: Reinventing the Real of Cinema." In *Alternative Projections: Experimental Film in Los Angeles, 1945–1980*, edited by David E. James and Adam Hyman, 163–174. New Barnet, UK: John Libbey Publishing, 2015.

Macdonald, Ian W. *Screenwriting Poetics and the Screen Idea*. New York: Palgrave Macmillan, 2013.

Maras, Steven. *Screenwriting: History, Theory and Practice*. New York: Wallflower Press, 2009.

Mekas, Jonas. *Movie Journal: The Rise of a New American Cinema, 1959–1971*. New York: Collier, 1972.

Millard, Kathryn. *Screenwriting in a Digital Era*. New York: Palgrave Macmillan, 2014.

Mouëllic, Gilles. *Improvising Cinema*. Amsterdam: Amsterdam University Press, 2013.

Movshovitz, Howie, ed. *Mike Leigh Interviews*. Jackson: University Press of Mississippi, 2000.

Murphy, J. J. *The Black Hole of the Camera: The Films of Andy Warhol*. Berkeley: University of California Press, 2012.

Murphy, J. J. "Looking through a Rearview Mirror: Mumblecore as Past Tense." In *A Companion to American Indie Film*, edited by Geoff King, 279–299. Chichester, UK: Wiley Blackwell, 2017.

Murphy, J. J. *Me and You and Memento and Fargo: How Independent Screenplays Work*. New York: Continuum, 2007.

Murphy, J. J. *Rewriting Indie Cinema: Improvisation, Psychodrama, and the Screenplay*. New York: Columbia University Press, 2019.

Naremore, James. *Acting in the Cinema*. Berkeley: University of California Press, 1988.

Nelmes, Jill, ed. *Analysing the Screenplay*. New York: Routledge, 2011.

Price, Steven. *A History of the Screenplay*. New York: Palgrave Macmillan, 2013.

Price, Steven. *The Screenplay: Authorship, Theory, and Criticism*. New York: Palgrave Macmillan, 2010.

Raphael, Amy, ed. *Mike Leigh on Mike Leigh*. London and New York: Faber and Faber, 2008.

Sawyer, R. Keith. *Improvised Dialogues: Emergence and Creativity in Conversation*. Westport, CT: Ablex Publishing, 2003.

Spolin, Viola. *Improvisation for the Theater: A Handbook of Teaching and Directing Techniques*. 3rd ed. Evanston, IL: Northwestern University Press, 1999.

Ward, Melinda, and Bruce Jenkins, eds. *The American New Wave, 1958–1967*. Minneapolis: Walker Art Center, 1982.

Index

Note: page numbers in *italics* refer to figures.